I Am Sion

No Better Wordz

I Am Sion

No Better Wordz

Sion

ASHFORD PUBLISHING

I AM SION

Copyright © 2013 by William Kitchen III

ISBN 978-0-976-99015-4 (softcover)

Books may be ordered from Ashford Publishing at
www.ellenashford.com
or from any quality book store in your area.

Manuscript assistant and editor: Lynn M. Scott

Photo restoration: Cecilia Brendel

Illustrations: Regi Hendrix

Book layout: John Beanblossom

Printed in the United States of America

In memory of my three Guardian Angels:
Houston and Helen Hughey
and Sebastain Hughey

This book is dedicated to
every voice that has been suppressed
and to every soul held captive

And to Houston Hughey II

And to Tina Bodley-Green, William C. Kitchen,
and Robert Earl Kitchen

And to my ancestors
who sacrificed their lives for my salvation

Contents

Acknowledgments

Allow me first to give eternal praise to the Most High God who continues to help me stand each time I fall.

In the same breath, I would like to give the highest honors to my mother, Renee Kitchen-McElrath, who has shown me undying love even when I felt I didn't deserve it. Words cannot describe the debt I owe you. Thank you for your love and loyalty. I love you, Ma. You are truly my best friend.

To the three Wise Men who have given me three different perspectives of fatherhood: William C. Kitchen II, Donald Walton, and Troy L. McElrath II.

William C. Kitchen II, my biological father with whom, through countless years of absence, I finally learned that his love for me is real and pure. No matter the struggles endured, I'll always be his son and love him.

Donald Walton, the first image of a dad I knew. He was there for me through thick and thin. Thank you and I love you.

Troy McElrath II, a man who extended a fatherly love to me day one. Thank you, Troy. Love you, man. Told you we're only going up from here.

I'd like to acknowledge my publisher, Ashford Publishing, who made my vision a reality. Thank you for your love and for this opportunity.

To Hasan, who carried the initial typing burden (with my mom). In addition, to Bob and Ora Hines, Mildred Johnson, Bernice Sydnor, and the late Linda Wooden for love and concern. To the late Pastor Stanley E. Ashford and the New Bethel Baptist Church, Beulah Baptist Church, Corinthians Baptist Church, Christ Temple Church, and Holy Trinity Church for keeping the power of Christ out front.

To N'cobra, NBUF, N.O.I, 5% and all other Black-conscious organizations who labor for the social and economic empowerment of Africans in this Diaspora.

I pay tribute to OG Mack and Pistol Pete and all the homies who held strong. To all the oppressed people who've rebelled against the status quo.

I also extend my honors to Michael E. Dyson, Na'im Akbar, Neal Rutherford, Charles X, Amen Ra, Dr. Cornell West, Struck, DeCarlose Smith, K-Travis El, Ben Chavis, Ra Saadi El, and Will "Rich Po" Coney. You brothers have directly or indirectly influenced my life in a positive way and have given me the essentials to develop into the man I am today.

To my Grandma Zora Kitchen and my Aunt Faye and Uncle Mitch Adams for making sure I had the books I wanted. To cousins Shaun, Shelon, Darrell, Darrion, Darrius, DeShawn, Ced, Dominique, David, and all the rest. To all my aunts and uncles, which to name everybody would call for a separate book to be written for that purpose alone. DT—What's Up?

I extend my sincerest love to Quintsey Jones (I told you), Melissa King, Shavon Pagget, Trisha Gorendal, Cherrel Doss,

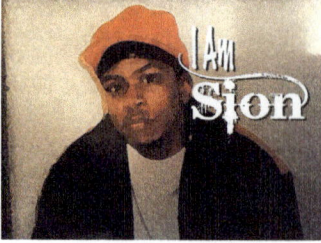

Chatin Briggs, and Tenesha Butler. I appreciate the friendship, past and present.

To my Blazin' Billys. This is to the Heights and every corner where we congregated. To every soul held captive, every voice that's been suppressed, every wrist that's ever been chained, to anybody who's ever been told they were a failure—this is for you.

To my adviser, Willie Coney, we did it, Brother. Word to the B-Hive: It's Pete 'til white sheet up.

SION

means

The name Sion is taken from the Biblical Zion.
Of its many definitions, it symbolizes Jerusalem,
which is a holy center for Jews, Christians, and Muslims.

I began referring to myself as Sion from a debate that was
sparked over the geographical location of Zion,
then expounded on it by evolving into the mentality of having a
name that resonated with Jews, Christians, and Muslims,
relating to a Universal Spiritual Connection.

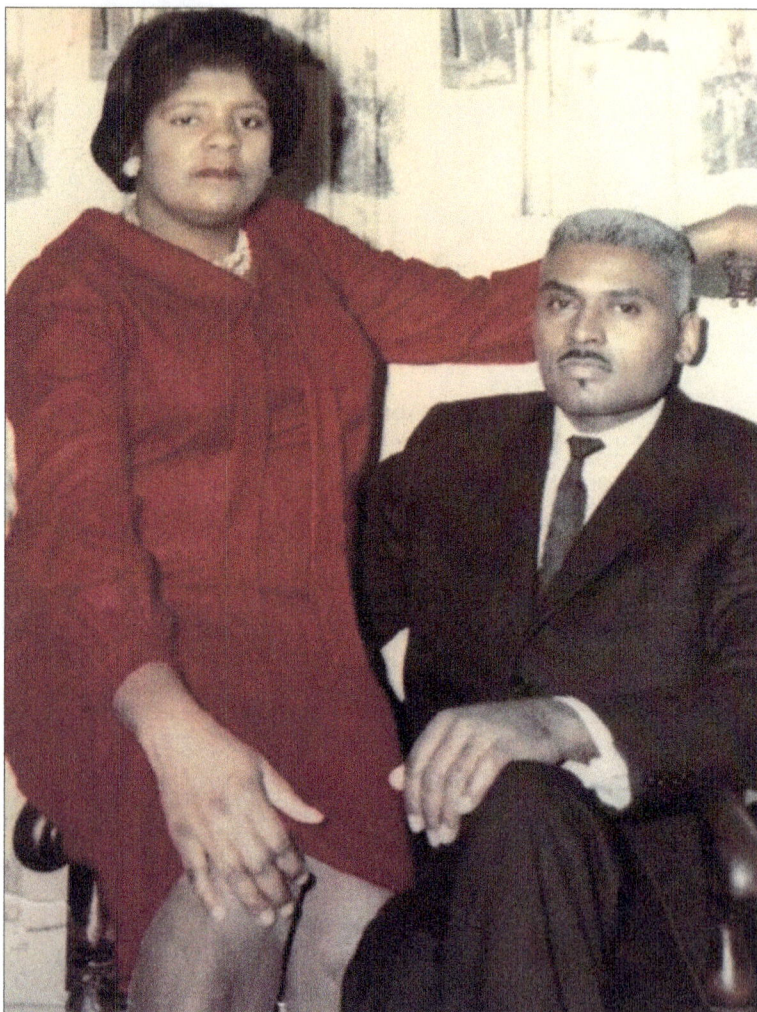

Photograph by Harrison Ashford

Helen Odessa Easter Hughey   8/08/1927 – 12/13/2008
Houston Hughey   10/21/1924 – 7/18/2001

My Grandparents

My grandparents came to the community of Muskegon Heights, Michigan, in 1947 from Waldo, Arkansas. Muskegon Heights is where they resided until their deaths.

My grandpa gained employment at CWC. He worked there for forty years. This was a factory that made motors for GM and Ford. On weekends he was a barber for many men and their young sons. During his cutting of hair, he gave advice, and he gave free haircuts to men who could not afford to pay the price. He did this until he was deathly sick.

My grandma was a licensed beautician. She worked in this position Tuesday through Saturday almost every week until her health began to deteriorate. She did this work for sixty-one years. I have seen my grandma give women in the community free hairstyles when she believed they could not pay. She also worked for the Muskegon Heights Public Schools as the lead lunch aide for eighteen years. She talked to students while she was serving lunch and reminded them that she knew their parents.

She and my grandpa joined the Beulah Baptist Church, where they were very faithful and active while raising their children.

There were many after-school sports, school bands, city sports, (YMCA, YFCA for boys and girls back in the day), boys' football, and baseball for the children in my family.

My mom said in their household all the children, boys and girls, had the same responsibilities. There were no girls' or boys' jobs.

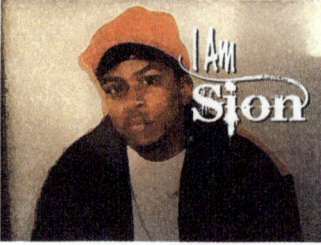

All of us were responsible for chores. This included everything from cleaning, cooking, mowing, shoveling, garbage detail, dishes washed, helping with laundry, and cleaning the beauty and barber shop, which was in their basement.

Grandpa did most of the after-school transportation maneuvering around town with the children. My uncle was learning to be a pharmacist and worked in a local drugstore. Under the direction of a licensed pharmacist, he was counting pills as my grandpa sometimes stood and watched proudly.

After-school activities were band concerts and baseball and city games. My aunts and uncles discussed how proud they were to have their family there watching them and cheering them on.

Grandma would be doing hair until about nine at night during the week. On weekends, my grandparents would get up about six in the morning and cook and serve breakfast. When the children were younger, they would be up and dressed early in the morning.

The housework was done before nine in the morning. My mom said she remembers her older sisters, Faye and Tina, helping out with the younger children.

Sometimes during the week and holidays, especially during Christmas, Thanksgiving, and Easter, my grandma would get someone to come in and help. These people were friends in our community. Mom said after all the things that went on with raising eight children, there was always room for more. This included cousins, aunts, uncles, and neighborhood children. They were always welcome at our house every day.

Mom said besides God, her children and her husband came first. She loved cooking. She cooked every day. On Fridays, that was Grandpa's day. The children knew what they were going to have for dinner. This included cream-style corn with hotdogs, rice, pork chops, apples, and milk. I remember how Grandma loved to cook and how much other people enjoyed her cuisine.

These are some of the foods I remember my grandma cooking (all homemade): goulash, spaghetti and meat balls, chili with cheese, rolls, biscuits, green peas and potatoes, green bean casserole, layer salads, yams, her baked beans, turkey and dressing, greens, macaroni and cheese, corn bread, scripture cake, pound cake, peach cobbler, blueberry pie with ice cream, Prince of Wales cake, banana pudding, coconut cake, German chocolate cake, peanut butter cookies, pecan pies, and home-made soups. OK, I am going to stop. Plus I'm making myself hungry.

As I think of the foods, I am also thinking of the poem I dedicated to her, "Don't Leave Me Now." She was chairperson over the kitchen at our church for eleven years.

When I was a child growing up, before I made the mistakes and landed in here, God blessed my grandparents at that time with sixteen grandchildren. We all had the privilege to know them. My grandparents did instill more in me than anyone would ever know.

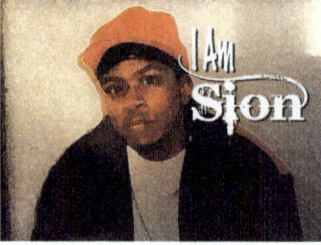

GHOST

The Introduction

Mom said I was a breach baby! It was said the day of my birth that I was trying to enter this world feet first, with the umbilical cord wrapped around my neck—hanging! Hey, I'm repeating what was told to me! I repositioned myself right before they performed a C-section, thus another "miracle baby" entered into this world.

I'm Mama's only child. None before me, none after me. Spoiled? Maybe, just don't call me a baby! My biological father, William, was distant. He had his own inner demons that he was dealing with. Donnie was my stepdad. Now I have Troy, doing for me what he can, when he can. He's not really social, but his love speaks volumes. Despite it all, my three dads have inspired my life and motivated my ambition for success. My biological father is no longer distant, and Troy is right here with me, but it's still just me and my mom.

The inner city of Muskegon Heights became my playground. I traded swings and slides for cigarettes and dice. I turned from a church boy into a street boy almost overnight. No more did I run through the corridors of the school hallways and churches. No, sir, I chose to run the street blocks.

Truthfully, my run was short, because in 2000, at the age of fourteen, I found myself in the Muskegon County Jail convicted of armed robbery and gun charges. I was sentenced to 11 to 40 years in prison, aka the pen, the big house, the bling, lockdown, the hole, the box, the damn CONCRETE CASKET!

I AM SION

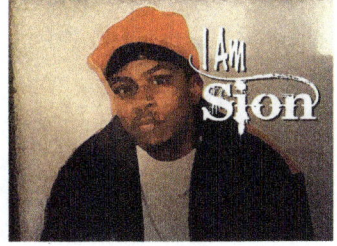

Though I was supposed to return to society in June 2011, my institutional behavior justified the parole board in giving me a "flop." This, simply put, is a delay on my release. During the last twelve years, I've endured much pain and anguish, though in every experience, there is a blessing and a curse. It's up to you which one you choose to extract.

So out of a curse I bring forth this blessing: a book of my thoughts and recollections, love and sorrow. In these pages, it was my intent to depict my life and feelings in words, painting a picture of the man I have become.

As of the date of this writing, I'm held in the hole of a maximum security prison. I surrender this book as a testament that, despite the odds and conditions of confinement, I EXIST, I LIVE.

I am that I am
SION
the Prince of Poetry

Renee Kitchen-McElrath

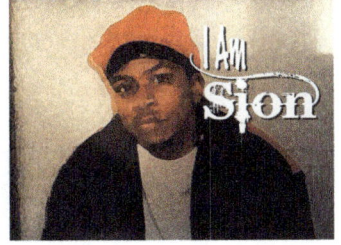

Chapter 1

How I See Things Now

"General opinion is no proof for truth,
for the generality of men are ignorant."

—Noble Drew Ali

DEAR RENEE

Carried him for nine months,
conceived him in pain,
From the labor she was drained,
as a result of the breach baby
that almost came.
William III he became,
Bubba he became,
unconditional love he was given.
He was his father's son
that gave her the love
she was missin'.

DEAR RENEE

Time can't measure
the words I want to say.
When Daddy was gone,
it was Daddy you had to play.
Even lying for him when I asked
why Daddy couldn't stay.
But you always kept love circulatin',
that's why I never questioned your love;
it was never up for debatin'.

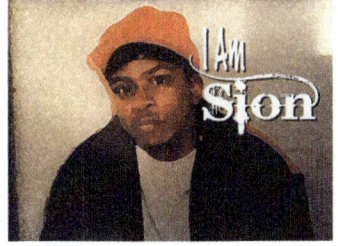

DEAR RENEE

I'm grateful I didn't have
to search for you.
If I could
I would bring the whole earth to you.
I wish I could've seen Helen's face
when she gave birth to you.
What a sight to have
seen Grandma's face
when she gave birth to you!

MY DEAR RENEE

QUICK QUESTION
What is the value of sacrifice?
What is it worth to you?
Cause ...
With one breath you gave me life
I appreciate you, SUPER MAMA!
Other mothers need to imitate you.
No birthday present, so this
TEAR DROP of love
is what I gave you.

DEAR RENEE

What else can I convey?
This is all truth—no lies.
When I'm in need of seeing Grandma,
I just look into your eyes.

DEAR RENEE

I love you like none other,
you are the perfect embodiment
of a mother.

DEAR RENEE

Forgive me for the
wrong that I've done;
For not meeting your expectations,
for not being a good son.

DEAR RENEE

Renee, my dear,
the end draws near.
Your loving words continue
to echo in my ear.
I wish I could ease
whatever troubles you.
KNOW THAT
through our ups and downs
I'm still loving you.

DEAR RENEE

In my last words
I wish to express
that I thank you so much
for doing your best.
My Dear Renee

A Letter to Oprah Winfrey

My Beloved Oprah,

If there ever was a name that could conjure greatness in my mind, it would be yours, Oprah Winfrey. There was a time in my past when I looked at you with childish eyes and considered you a sellout. I would think to myself about having your type of money and all the beautiful and progressive contributions I would make for the reconstruction of inner-city dwellings, about all of the people of my race that I could aid, and all of the people of my community that I could show the world to.

Many of my contemporaries felt, and even probably still feel, that you're not doing what you should or what you could do with YOUR money. Now, with much more mature thoughts, I ask myself why they/we are so concerned with YOUR money and how YOU decide to spend it. The truth is, as I sit here in a state of captivity, I've arrived at the understanding that most of us had an opportunity to have YOUR type of money. However, we often-times choose different means of acquiring our finance and ways that may not always have been legal. Either that or we didn't know how to manage our money, even though we may not have had YOUR tenacity and desire.

I truly believe at this point in my life that out of all the success and fame you've earned, you are still underrated. Your contributions to our race and humanity as a whole are greatly underestimated. I had to face the harsh reality that while I criticized you for your efforts to advance the quality of our people, I sit here in prison for hurting them; that while you continue to prove

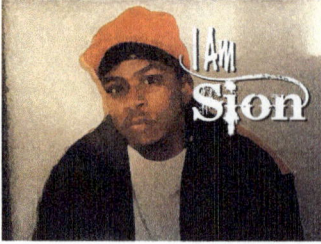

to be a positive force in our culture's enhancement, I have proven to be only a detriment.

So forgive me, because the man in me today appreciates your struggle and understands that because you have had to struggle, you've saved countless others from having to experience that struggle for themselves. I'm grateful to you for showing the world the meaning of diversity and giving our people an image of creativeness and greatness.

My love for you, Oprah, is undying.

Truly,

Sion

I AM SION

AL – PROLIFIC SUPREME

THE MOVEMENT

WARNING SHOTS

EPIC

My pen is my sword,
I can give life
or bring death with it.
Cause birth with language
or departure with lyric.

Practicing lyrical sorcery
my vernacular conjures
the hidden force in me.
Forcing me
to let this ink bleed
and my pens cry.
I can cut 'em deep
before the ink dries,
injure 'em
before the paper stains.

Because my thoughts are ammunition,
they manifest for visual.
The bloodshed has arisen
from a massacre with words.
With a composition that's poetic—
literal but allegoric—
optimistic but prophetic,
multi-dimensional
but incomprehensible
to a mind that's pathetic,
either that or synthetic!

Let it
be known
that this isn't poetry,
it's epic!

My words are constructed
in sequence.
We are just
urban regents, poetic legions,
in genius in every season,
masters of our mental regions.
Proceed with this
and be astonished!
Despite what you believe in—
be it!

A stranger to the author
who is enlightened when they read this.
I'm respected from a distance
because my words are in precedence—
I mean precedence.

I told you this was epic
as far as confessions went!

REINCARNATION

Reincarnation got me seeing things clearly,
because rebirth of the past
is an eye opener that stirs me—
born again, new body, same soul,
meaning purified—
different life, same goal.

SUCCESS

Is truly what I yearn.
Failure in a different form
is what caused me to return
unto this life as a bird
flying opposite the winds.
Rather battle for my place
than be blown in where the end begins.
I predate the first sin,
My soul has been recycled time and again.

Immersed in primordial waters,
taught by the elders,
walked with the Biblical fathers,
conceived hieroglyphics—I'm a stone carver!

I AM SION

I'm each and everything
the mind possibly thought of—
from justice to hate—
all rooted by work and love,
boxing the opponent
centuries before Golden Glove.

Perpetually spoken of
by nations of every tongue,
conceptually my name hung.
My breath became the wind
and my soul became the sun.

I was the first breath that incarnated
into the flesh,
then that ceased
so I reincarnated into the next.
Then I figured when I transfigured
that the body is just a vehicle
that secures the holy breath.
Reincarnation.

AL-PROLIFIC SUPREME

Every inch and moment
I live as a poet,
me and millions of others
who don't even know it.
Cause I show it.
Eternity is what I reap
simply because I sowed it.
Al-Prolific Supreme—
displaying epics as a faction,
creating universal disturbances
when thought combines with action.
Digest with your mind,
and now make your mental pores hot.
You can't label me as a poet;
I'm a poetic warlock!

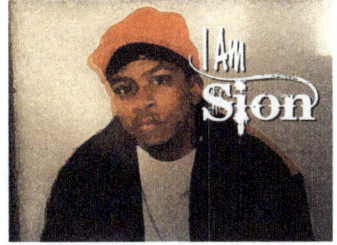

CONTROVERSY

There can never be a toss-up
between APS and someone else
because I'm the root of all of the feelings
that I've felt.
If you believe I spit riddles,
then use enigma to enforce me,
and you'll force my incantation
through this lyrical sorcery.

Then the spell will take its toll
until the enemy starts rehearsing,
Al-Prolific Supreme
instigating controversy.
But then again you won't beat 'em
and only inflict self-tragedy,
so respect poetic majesty
usin' dialectic rhapsody.

Poetic Teacher, Poetic Learner,
Poetic Massacre, Poetically Nat Turner,
Telepathy—third eye seer.

Motivated by those who doubt me,
word to Angelia,
I'm in conflict with an angel,
I guess it makes me a demon.

If God is the subject,
then it makes me the meaning—
controversy.

POETIC IMPOSTERS ARE AT MY MERCY

Supreme the Creator; either that or cremator,
you frauds are vampires and I'm a Poetic Slayer. Talkin'
but you ain't sayin' nothin',
poetic head-huntin' devoured 'em.
Stomach still grumblin'; lyrical warfare
but all they doing is mumblin'.

They don't really like us, we too controversial;
It's not our fault those other poets
need better rehearsal.

Cause my violets ain't blue and my roses ain't red;
my knuckles are bloody and my lil' homie is dead.

I only speak what I know; quote what I feel.
The ghetto left scars
and those wounds will never heal.

Disconfigure ya' tongue,
I give instructions to the sun.
I'm speakin' now, you can speak when I'm done.
I'll plunge my sword into you liars;
this flamin' word that was purged in holy fire.

I AM

The universal sire, so who am I to these poets?
Their father? No, not a role model!
Cause they can't show it,
Just notice the backfire when my words are recited.

Flame is ignited—examine the paper
And watch the words as they write it;
my mind is a blow torch,
my pen is a flame thrower of truth.
I'm a freight train
with scorched poets in my caboose.

I respect spoken words,
but not those reciting it;
with these sparks I'm ignitin' it.
Took this poetry and put my fuckin' life in it,
APS masters these poets too passive!
You got questions? Well, we got answers.

They say they are poets, but they don't live it;
manifested truth depicted my thoughts vivid.
They ask what makes Al-Prolific Supreme?
I tell 'em three gods existing as one being.

ALLURE

Infatuated with her scent,
obsessed with her smile;
one is intoxicating,
the other will astound—
so I'm intoxicated
by the woman that I'm around.
Her aura so profound,
impossible to abscond.

I lay with her physically,
I walk with her mentally,
connect with her intimately,
we're tied through chemistry.
Every tendency complementary
on the same page, defying symmetry.

Massage her brain, stimulate her pulse.
She's intrigued, so I arouse her thoughts;
made love to her mind.
Organic eruptions, eternal combustions;
in the essence of time,
in the substance of consciousness.
Resting in a silky place, her infinite grace
outstretches the Milky Way;
so damn comforting.

I AM SION

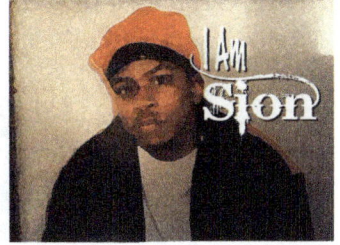

Like a touch of a mother, a voice so soothing
that contemplates no other,
her larynx's vibration projects audible art;
artfulness to a god,
a creation from the heart.

Apart from parables and metaphors,
I'm in perpetual pursuit
of that beauty that allures.

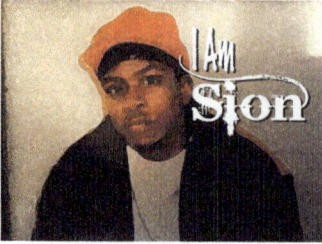

RHYTHM

Rhythm is actually larger than self;
every pulse, every thought, every step.
I heard vibratory pitches
even as I slept.
Death is a time of mourning,
as quiet as kept.
People crying to my right,
even more to my left.
I saw sorrow,
but still heard melody as they wept.
Except
that the facts of this storyline remain,
leaves extracting water
roam the passage of the rain.
The drops and drizzles
create puddles inside crevices;
melodic footsteps
sounding as if the winds and songs are mixing.

Walking turns into jogging,
his right arm slices to his hip,
draws like a Western,
holds on with arm-wrestling grip.
The pursued freeze as the pursuer squeezes.

I AM SION

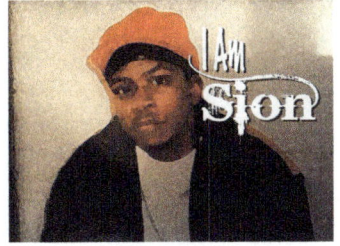

The fire pin that was squeezed
enables the ballistics,
ejects the hollow tips
from the magazine
as the muzzle spits
through the flesh as it hits it;
sounds like a clap
whose syncopation doesn't stick.
Screams come operatic,
followed by bass as he falls;
the rhythms of life begin,
when the singing of death calls.

So rhythm, yes rhythm,
actually larger than self,
every pulse, every thought, every step,
I heard vibratory pitches even as I slept.

MY NAME IS?

It's the cipher that depicts this.
The Romans called my soul invidious.
Whatever's in the bearings of my presence I expose?
From times before ancient times I arose.
I'm nothing but celestial; I'm omnipresent,
and I love earth the same as I'd love a crescent.
I was when man wasn't! That's recorded truth!
Life is evolution, but to me it's nothing new.
Me and heaven are related, the stars are my
closest kin; from Mercury to Pluto,
the planets are my friends.
I symbolize the Asiatic
and shine the paths of his feet.
My female relatives fill in when I'm asleep.
I rest in the west land, the earth gives me feast,
but Africa's the first I greet.
I awake in the east, all nations love my existence,
some even worship me,
and thru each and all battles
I keep my peace.
Rather war, tragedy, or disaster,
I always have a smile;
my swag illuminated, the truth is my style.

I AM SION

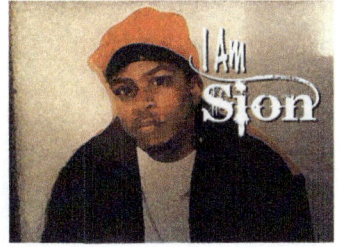

Mankind causes havoc,
but shun during my eclipse,
when in actuality,
I was only meeting the moon for a bit.
I come as I AM and as I AM, I go.
Projecting unrestrained love,
and all love will glow.
I'll be with you when you lose
and be the same when you've won.
It's nice to meet you, world …
my name is the sun!

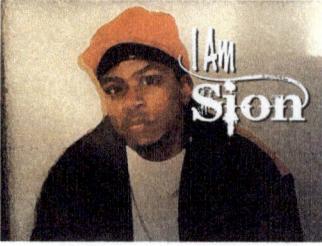

ANOINTED

Submerged in ancient corridors,
no torch lit.
The only light is the gleam
from my amulet.

I wager my life,
play with death—gamble with it.
If you knew you had the power of god
could you handle it?

Existence being at your command;
"I command you to live!"

POETIC SUPREMACY

Unconsciously
this world has been impatiently
waitin' for the reign of a kingdom.
It's exasperatin'.
So we're excavatin'
into the poetic realm for escalation.
Don't worry, this is the inauguration.

Embarking on a new mission
my soul was transmitted through
parallel dimensions;
you've waited for this day
to be mentioned.

Don't forget who brings it—
every poet is hunted.
Cut open their nuclei
and spit in their stomach.
Fire has arrived,
leaving poets in the mortar,
carving their Adam's apple
so they can't speak with water.

Lingual mastery
possessed by lyrical masters;
tragically but masterfully
burying poet masters.

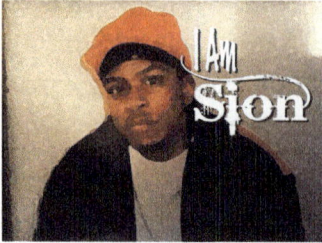

I control the scene
when elevated mind controls me;
the commander of verbs,
commanding words through poetry,
I speak with increased potency.
Poetic visions
trying to extract the little hope in me,
from the third person,
inspired by those quotin' me.

Collect my thoughts,
then construct my words.
Grand architect
when it comes to composing words.
My words will penetrate your body
and pinch your nerves.
Switch verbs and instruct nouns,
levitate off the ground
and meditate on poetic sound;
it's difficult to stand around.
Poetic supremacy starts now!

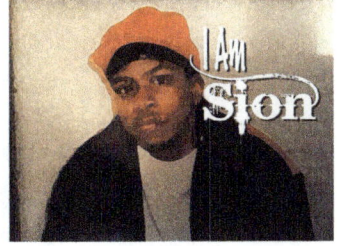

DATE WITH DESTINY

Standing face to face,
eyes meant to intimidate,
but his thoughts wondered
how he got to this place;
stopped in his tracks
with a gun in his face!

The gunman didn't want to pull it,
but he feared for his life,
and in his memory he knew
what he had done that night.

FIRST LET'S TRAVEL IN REVERSE
Nature's trigga' hand
no longer extended—
easing back to his waist,
securing the 40-cal
back in its place.
Will moving backward
before he seen Lama.
He uttered the words
"You killed Imma!"
Were those the words he chose?
Back through the door;
knobs turn, doors close—
time froze!!

Now to the placement of the prison;
Will did fifteen although he was innocent.
Robbed of his freedom
so he hasn't forgotten it;
charged with a murder
that he never committed.

Couldn't wait to see his daughter
and even his baby's mother;
but never again.

Will she be the same Karma?
Anxiety and excitement
were written on Will's face!
He stepped out and was embraced
by Destiny and Nate.
He looked in the girl's face
and saw that time had gone.
Biggest hug possible—
her silence played a joyous song!
Will paused and looked
at the young man,
then Nature said, "Nice to meet you!"
and extended his right hand.

The formalities were over;
they returned to the neighborhood.
Nature put his car in park
when they entered Karma's house.
It was for a talk.

I AM SION

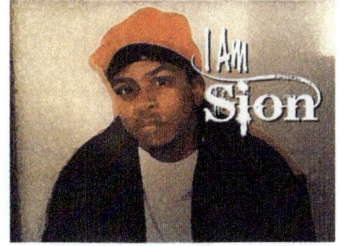

Nature sat quiet;
Destiny took the lead.
The boy put his eyes on his shoes,
sweaty-handed palms on his jeans.

She said,
"Dad, I hate mom!"
Karma's random men and drugs,
and until I found Nature,
I had never felt loved.

She cried while Will thought;
Nature did as he was taught;
To never interfere with such moments,
so he left to take a walk.

Now that Will heard the story
of the role that Nature had played,
he respected Nate as a man
and began to prepare for the party
that Destiny had planned.

The party lasted for a while,
but being amongst the elders
wasn't really Nate's style.
So he and Destiny left
right before it was over.
Nature lived across
the street from Karma
and a couple of houses over.

Will watched Destiny depart,
and smiled at the only one
who had ever had his heart.
Nature walked hand in hand
with Destiny
'til they arrived at his spot.
Nature had planned
to get Destiny hot.
See, she was a virgin
and for two months,
Nate had been urgin',
sexual flirtin'.

But she was only sixteen
and wasn't interested in birthin' babies;
but Destiny never knew about
those other ladies.
That night Nature got crazy!

Hoping to lure her
into his sexual persuasion;
kissin' and grindin' on the couch—
hormones ragin'.

Destiny loved Nature,
she was willing to take a chance;
so her virgin hands
started moving in his pants.
In his mind he knew that it was time,
so he whispered to Destiny,
"Baby be mine."

48

But it was something about his words
that made her hesitate,
then turn away, finally convey,
"I can't do this, sorry Nate."
He was in the moment
and Nature couldn't wait—
so Nature had his way!

He wouldn't get off
and before she knew it,
her clothes were ripped off.
Her body pinned to the couch,
he thrust inside and she cried out,
"Please, don't do this!
Nature, please stop!"
Face contorted from fear,
struggle along with shock,
hoopin' and hollarin'
givin' his chest ragin' knocks.
So he smacked her in the mouth,
she silently took stock.

Destiny's hands clasped together,
forced against her chest.
Her head turned toward
the Jesus picture
while he tightly gripped her neck!
In disbelief thinkin' about the regrets,
with rabid pain in her vagina
and thriving aches in her breasts.

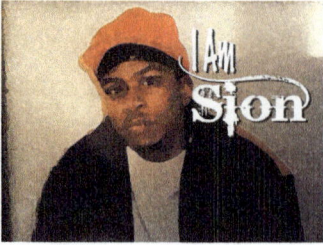

It was many times she witnessed
her own mother selling sex—
but a victim of rape?
She hadn't imagined being next!

Ironically she relaxed;
she looked up at Nature
and to her surprise
he was still violently strokin',
cursin' her with despise.
She was numb but felt liberated
as he abandoned his disguise,
and all she said was
"WHY?"
With tear-stained cheeks
she stared murderously in his eyes.
He said, "SHUT the hell up and
let Nature have his way!"
The circumstances remained.

As he leaned forward and kissed her
the moment that he came,
he didn't seem remorseful.
But finally self-conscious
she laid there for a second
until she felt the vomit.

She slyly tucked her phone
and staggered quickly
to the bathroom.
First thing she saw was her reflection—
face swollen as a balloon

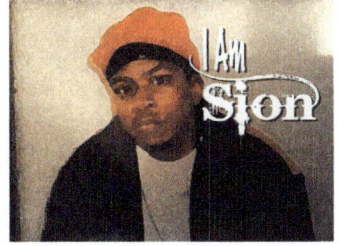

with the feeling of maroon.
The gagging never made it,
but that was Nature's doom.

Her womanhood was in scorn
and so was her pride;
sitting hopelessly on the toilet,
blood racing down her thighs.
She had to decide—
hide it or fight against the faults?
So with all the strength she could muster,
Will dominated her thoughts.

This reality was traumatized,
now that Nature had destroyed her wall.
Free Will had been callin' Destiny,
now she'd return the call.

Her eyes began to swell
with the rain from within her own storm,
the Sunshine will come
before more clouds can form.
At least that's what she had been told
by the face that's in her locket,
that was her Grandmother Charm
who said only God could stop it.

She always talked with Destiny
and told her she'd be fine,
But there was an inescapable doubt
that had entered into her mind.

As she searched through her thoughts,
what kind of answer would she find?
Now she knew the meaning
of David's Psalm 59.

Her whole body trembled
as she moved across the floor,
making sure Nate didn't hear her
open the bathroom door.

Simultaneously Nature searched for Destiny,
still drunk from spirits he said,
"I owe you for scratching me!"
Yelling from room to room,
sure to hurt her wherever he found her.
By the time Will arrived,
she was hiding beneath the kitchen counter.
The knob turned, the door opened, and in an instant,
Will heard the sound of Nature
thrashing in the distance.

Will crossed the threshold
in pursuit of the voice,
he got nearer, and the living room
was his first choice.

I AM SION

Standing face to face,
his eyes meant to intimidate,
but his thoughts wondered
how he got to this place?
It's crazy the cards Destiny will deal you,
but his daughter was his concern
so he said, "I'm gonna kill you!"

Nate pulled the 40-cal. from his waist;
he feared for his life.
He knew the reality
of what he had done that night.

Destiny felt strange
as she peered from beneath the counter
and witnessed the whole exchange.
She was scared and conflicted in her thoughts,
but seeing the gun pointed at her father,
she made her move on impulse.

She crawled from beneath the counter,
hid on the side of the stove.
All in one blink
she semi-stood and pulled the knife
from the kitchen sink.

She swung around the corner
and was facing the back of Nature
so she was able to see
the eyes of her Savior.

He saw her too!
Will was now more scared
than he had ever knew;
but anger began to rise as he noticed
Destiny's blood and her swollen eyes.

Will started approaching Nature,
like "What's this about?"
At the same time Nature was steppin' back,
like "Nothing to talk about."

Will didn't want to scare him,
so he didn't shout. He just
said all he had to say—
"I come for Destiny,
and I'll be on my way."

Nature kept steppin' back,
told Will to stop where he's at.
Will obliged
as tears fell from Nate's eyes.

Now Destiny stood five feet away
contemplating the risk
as she held the butcher's knife
that was clutched in her fist.

I AM SION

Nature pulled the hammer back—
time frozen.
Destiny's eyes snapped open,
she then understood
the path that was chosen.

Nature told Will, "I got no choice left,"
neither did Destiny
as she plunged the knife
into Nature's neck.

Nate jerked
and his finger twitched.
Nate fell
and Will said, "Shit!"

Nate was stabbed in his neck and
that caused the bullet to be ejected;
in Will's chest
the hollow tip was inflicted.

Will dropped to his knees,
looking dead at Destiny;
Nature altered fate with Will,
and Karma was the recipe.

Slowly Will fell back,
his hands placed against his chest.
Blood gushing from his wound,
so he pressed and compressed.

Destiny rushed to her father,
bewildered, but no screaming,
hoping to awake from this nightmare
that she was dreaming.

Destiny held Will, both his legs under his back;
head cradled in her hands, arms around his neck.
When she looked into his eyes, tears started to well,
but weeping wouldn't help, and Destiny could tell.
She said very firmly, "Daddy, I'm callin' 911!"
He just stared into space and more tragedy began.

Destiny was stuck as she called the police;
pulled from reality into a world of disbelief.
Nature had slumped over the couch,
his face held a grimaced smirk.
The knife fell, Destiny jumped,
then blood started to squirt.

All of a sudden Will spoke!
"No room for cryin' baby,
you're my DESTINY
and a good reason for dyin.'"

Karma came around
but felt the least bit of worry
as the medics bagged Nate's body and
carried Will's out on a gurney.
This isn't the end yet, but a very movin' story.

When Nature abuses free Will,
Karma's cycle becomes Destiny's journey.

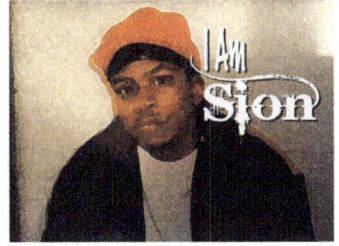

Will's funeral was touching,
Nature's was detested;
despite his life on earth,
the deceased was well respected.

Life goes on.
Destiny again lives dejected;
until she has a checkup,
and finds out she's pregnant!

Grandma Charm came from Georgia
and took Destiny in with open arms,
Charm still had twenty years left in her,
so Destiny wasn't alarmed.

Only every so often she thought back
to some of her worst days,
but Destiny looked forward to giving birth
in the hours of her own birthday.

She never thought she'd want this,
but what's done can't be changed.
There's no undoing DESTINY,
when DESTINY has its date.

All bad stories don't end badly,
and here's the reason why,
because out of all of KARMA'S wrongdoing,
DESTINY borne HOPE!

I AM GOD

Be and it is.
Like giving life to a form
or bringing death with narcotics,
to a God it's mechanics,
to a mortal it's robotics.

The master of kinematics,
user of kinetics,
the professor of phonics,
the inventor of phonetics.
PATHETIC.
Can you be God?
And not know you're a genius?
Knowledge, wisdom, understanding;
I advise you to seek this.
Recognized by all of humanity,
you're the prefix.
I demise
then emerge from the flames—Phoenix!

A new-found Christ
reminding me of my own stigma,
these revelations are engraved
in my psyche—this enigma.
No manipulation needed,
breathing is charisma.

I AM SION

Every word lingers
with more effect than a parable,
but if your mentality is shallow,
the profundity will tear you.
Vocals of freight, a voice of hypnotic,
reality in itself,
expressed clearly, symbolic.

I play with death,
so my life I gamble with,
I have the power that God gave me,
and this is one way that I handle it.

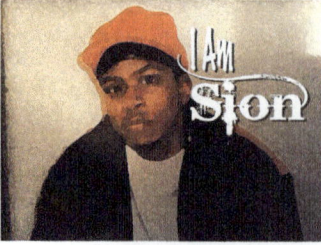

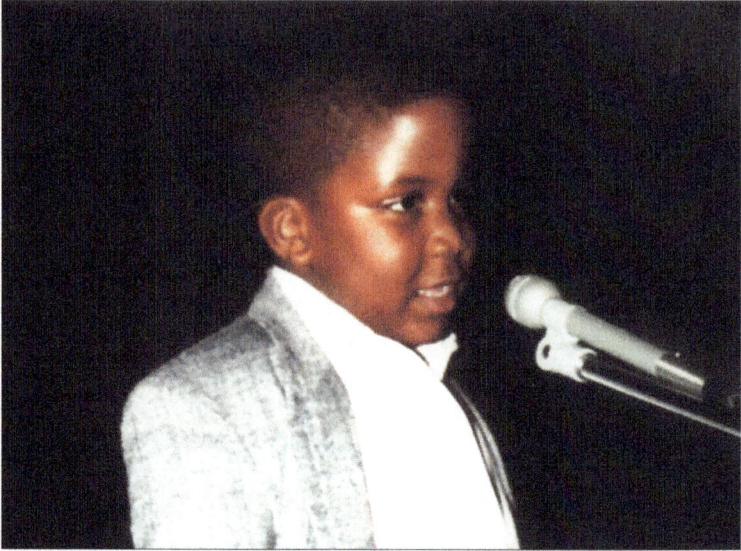

Since I was about seven years old, I can remember being given poems to recite at church during the holiday events. I can remember always appreciating the beauty of words and how you could reach so many people with them.

Chapter 2

Reflections

"Whilst we deliberate how to begin a thing,
it grows too late to do it."

—Quintilian

She Cries for You

There was a time in Africa when Africans became subjected to Arab-European subjugation, when European captors sought to inflict the harshest and cruelest pain imaginable on the captive male slave. Though that enslaved male knew if he turned his head to the side, he would find the face of a beautiful African sister with whom he could share a tear.

While in the depth of that darkened and crowded slave ship, where bodies were cramped side by side, and in many cases on top of one another—destination North America—slaves were chained, beaten, and forced to sit and lie in puddles of their own excrement. Although suffering from such neglect, the enslaved male knew that if he searched that large black box, he would catch the eye of that same African sister, glistening with liquid tears as she too cried with him.

Upon arriving to a foreign land, hearing a language unknown to him, seeing people who he considered "kinless," he was pranced around naked, not knowing that he had been passed off from the hands of a "slave captor" to those of a "slave trader," and soon, for the right price, he would be sold to a "slave owner." "SOLD" was the word he heard, but didn't comprehend its meaning. Off he went! Still, as he picked up his lowered head, he found the face of that same African sister who cried with him as they carried him away.

Then the dreaded day came when the master wanted to make an example out of him to the other slaves. The master, in the glory of his cowardice, took that whip and swung it a dozen

times, stretching each agonizing lash across the slave's back. The slave cried deeply, ashamed and beaten, lying there feeling defeated. Until he felt those small, tender hands nursing his wounds and, before he could muster enough strength to open his eyes, he felt the salty tears of that same African sister drop onto his body. He knew, although barely conscious, that she was crying with him.

After he was emancipated, at least physically, he struggled to find employment. Only having the job skills of a slave, the "free" Negro was forced to work for slave wages. Unable to provide for his family, he broke down and cried. He cried for injustice! He cried for discrimination! He cried for all the times he had never cried! Then he looked up into his wife's eyes and saw the reflection of his soul and knew that her tears were produced from his pain. She cried with him.

Then, with the passing of time, through his consumption of drugs and his manifested desire for white women, he had forgotten the pain, he had forgotten with whom he had shared his tears! The beautiful African sister had somehow become a BITCH! Who wants a BITCH? Times had changed, he had changed, and his tears had all dried up. The sad reality isn't that he doesn't cry anymore, it's that if you look into the eyes of that BEAUTIFUL African sister, she no longer cries with you, SHE CRIES FOR YOU!

I AM SION

Grew up without a pot,
didn't know what to piss in.
My mother was my father
'cause my daddy never pitched in.
I used to blame him,
now I understand him.
Love him still,
even when I can't stand him.

It's a cold world,
but I think we're even.
Put me against death,
and I'll come out swingin'.
What am I thinkin'? I'm bilingual,
can you decipher the meanin'?
Tribal kin'
so those conservative ladies
found me intriguin'.
I conjure ancient curse,
recite the Quran;
bleed over Biblical verses.
So—
I make salaam on Fridays,
and on Sundays
congregate in the churches.

I AM SION

Told you—
I speak with different tongues;
affiliated with Muslim,
converse with nuns.

Categorically?
I'm not to be placed in a category.
Many have misplaced
the same with the glory.

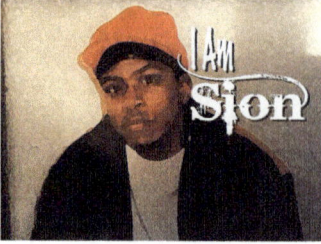

I AM SION

This is the truest story.
Fatherly love?
I never felt that fatherly love.
Hell, for a long time
I didn't even know what a father was!
Just a mother, grandpa, and grandma,
cause Father was gone
before I was even out of my Pampers.

Many years I cried for you,
but there was no ear to listen.
Where were you?
I was being raised by a prison!
Don't think I'm speaking out of anger;
you gave me your name,
yet you remain a stranger.
For a long time I thought I was a waste,
felt I was the reason
that we couldn't live in the same place.
Vented my aggression,
Father, here's a little taste.

Questioning my own self, like
why should I even bother?
Maybe because none of us is perfect,
and the man is my father.

Apologies are due. How can I resent you?
Why would I degrade you?
If we never speak again,
know that your son appreciates you.

THROUGH MY EYES

Through my eyes
I reside where ...
convicts are convicted without evidence,
where injustice is evident,
and the words "fuck the police"
are prevalent.

Where they seek to entomb you
in a concrete casket,
and even predators become
victims to torture tactics.

This can't be my reality!
SADLY
I compose this analogy;
that I know many doing
life sentences on a technicality.

See, I've seen boys come in and
grow into men; then
think they're girls
and turn to men.
This can't be my end!
Can't adopt prison normalcy,
can't blend in.

So I stand out,
chin up—chest out!
I will not be defeated,
will not be weakened!
Solid—five days a week
and extra on the weekend!

I RISE
In the midst of lies
to merely give you a glimpse
of life through my eyes.

ALL I'VE KNOWN

Pain!

Tell me—can you feel this pain?

Shame!

Have you ever felt this shame?

I remember when the verdict came in and the gavel a-banged.

In that moment, I knew things would never be the same.

Journey with me back down memory lane …

They say my birth was a blessin';
that I shouldn't have made it past conception.

My mother had a broken marriage, that relationship she eluded.

'Cause the love she gave my father, he seldom abused it.

Pops lived around the corner, but he was so distant,
searching for happiness in all of the wrong places.

I grew up with insecurities written on my face;
internally I was hurtin' but my mother couldn't see it.

She was always working,
so by the streets I was groomed.

2000 was the year, second week of June.
I think the curse of my life came too soon.

When have I ever tried to do harm?
Shots fired! Charges—robbery and firearm.
14 years old—convicted.
11 to 40 years to a kid—are you kiddin'?

Sorry to my mother. I know the mothers feel it.
I'll be home soon, Lord willing.

Though I'm still standing in a prison cell and all,
knuckles bloody from punching these walls.

For a minute I was lost in the crowds of sorrow
of those I write about in these sentences.

Why support a judicial system that locks up babies
for mandatory minimum sentences?

Come to prison a child, leaving a grown man,
nothing to my name but a pocket full of sand—bringing me shame.

I used to scream out daily, now I can't even muffle a sound.

My voice suppressed, no empathy for those oppressed.

It's just sad to know that we're standing alone,
and it's difficult for me to fight to return back home.

Been here since I was 14,
this is all I've known.

THE CHILD CRIES

Why does the child cry?
He cries for he has seen his fate
and knows that the absence of love
has produced nothing but hate.

The child cries
for a life he once had;
a life once known.
He cries for the father
he has never known.

The child cries.
He does so for
the wounds created by memories.
The heart detects
the spirit's injuries—
their inquiries.

Why does the child cry?
For the pain he brought to another,
for gambling with life,
for hurting his mother.

The child cries
repetitive tears;
never conquered, repeated fears.
Years have passed,
but the tears, they last—
shamed by insecurities.

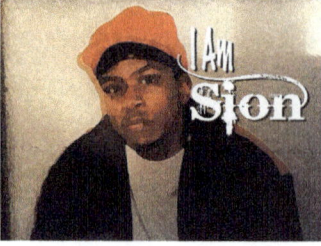

Whether he wears a mask,
it doesn't hide his cries;
it barely conceals the lie.
For it lies deep,
so the child cries,
cries himself to sleep.

The child cries,
but it isn't sympathy
he's requesting;
it's empathy he questions.

He cries for untaught lessons,
casts curses to heaven;
feelings he never received
his promised blessings.

The child cries,
though there are no ears to listen.
How many children go unheard
because they're crying from prison?

HOW I SEE IT

See, I used to cast stones
at the church house,
the preacher bored me.
Called Jesus on the mainline,
felt like he ignored me.
Tried to talk with Mom,
she was too busy to listen.
With Pops in exile,
I was literally raised by the prison.
I've reached the lowest depths,
regardless of how I see Jesus,
I felt his pain when he wept.

I admit I was Mama's baby,
then I turned defiant
and drove my mama crazy.
Accustomed to the storm,
so the rain don't phase me.
Yes, you can see the pain on my face.
Believe me,
I drink my own tears
to see how my pain tastes.
I move constantly,
but I'm still stuck in the same place.

So now I measure time
and calculate my place.
Believe it! Life is a fairy tale,
according to how I see it.

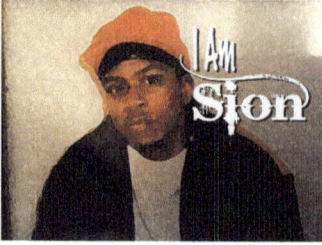

For Q!

The illusions of them aiding me
only offend me.
Lost in an uncaged prison
where no one seems to
comprehend me.
I dwell within frustration and pain.
It feels as if all that education has been in vain.

The path I've taken
has led me to nowhere
but feeling empty inside.
God hasn't been found
where I thought he would reside.

I do not know
what tomorrow may bring,
or even if I'll be here
to greet the sun.
I no longer have hope—
nothing ... none!

I try and fight it,
but the depression fights back.
The stress moves so swiftly,
before my conscious mind
can even react.

They say they love me,
but there's no love felt.
They only voice criticism,
no one really tries to help.

So I sit here,
just my thoughts and I.
Consistently posing questions
to myself like,
What if? and Why?

I'm hurting day after day,
months have turned into years.
Life's a bitch, and I didn't
ask to be here!

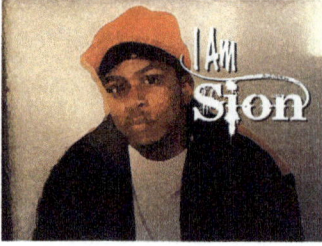

DON'T LEAVE ME NOW!

Don't leave me now!
If there ever was a moment—
I need you now.
I wish joy could return,
someway, somehow.
Grandma, promise—
you won't leave me now.
I have so much love to repay,
so I hope God doesn't
perceive this as being selfish,
but "I" need you to stay.
So does Trea, Missy, and Renee,
and what about Dwight,
Butchy, and Faye?
Please don't leave me now!

But if you shall depart
before I arrive,
Trust that I'll keep your spirit alive.
For and through you
I shall always breathe,
it is because of you
that I still believe.
The only thought
worthy to conceive
is in the form of a prayer,
that you will never leave.

DON'T LEAVE ME NOW!

IS MY EYES RED?

Is my eyes red?
I haven't slept in days,
those days feel like weeks.
Nor have I eaten,
maybe that's why my body
feels so weakened.

Is my eyes red?
I've been crying a lot lately.
Haven't heard from my friends,
and wondering, do they hate me?
Have they forgave me
for indulging in that substance
that made me
act a little crazy?

IS MY EYES RED?

They just ought to be.
It's my birthday,
and nobody thought of me.
No text messages,
no calls for me.
Is my eyes red?
See what they causin' me?
Is my eyes red?
Bloodshot, I tell you.
Crucified nightmares,
to the cross they will nail you—
sorry I failed you.
MY EYES IS RED!

The Zodiac

Chapter 3

Love

"There is only one kind of love,
but there are a thousand imitations."

—Francois de La Rochefoucauld

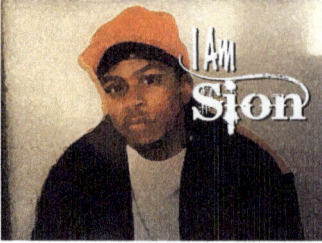

A Letter to My Mother

Dear Renee,

I don't even know where to begin. For as long as I can remember, you've always stood by me, never wavered, no matter the struggle. As far as I'm concerned, I've never been the best son to have, but you always embraced me, never stopped loving me, even when I stopped loving myself. Through the last couple of years, I've questioned if I truly deserve someone like you in my life. You've done and sacrificed so much for me that I've felt as if I'm not worthy of such love.

You are the perfect friend, my best friend. No one on this earth can ever come close in comparing to you. When my days grow dark, I think of you for light. When I consider failure, you won't allow it. At one point I contemplated death, but you gave me reason to live. At times I try to differentiate you from the billions of mothers across the globe. I wouldn't trade you or have you any other way.

You've given me so much, but what have I given you? I've brought you so much pain. What have I done to make you proud? I've done nothing but take your love for granted. You deserve to have a successful lawyer or doctor for a son, a son that you can brag about. How can you ever brag about your son, the convicted felon? I've given you nothing!

So as I write this letter, please know that I'm sorry. Sorry for the sleepless nights, sorry for the tears, sorry for each time that I've broken your heart. I'm sorry for the disappointments, sorry for not listening, I'm truly sorry for embarrassing you. I'm sorry for

spending so much of your money, and I'm sorry for every time I've had to say sorry.

But I'll tell you this—I've found life through this pen, and with it I'll write our future and change my stars. It's not yet over, and I intend to create my own destiny. When it's all said and done, you'll be proud and happy to call me your son.

MY PEN BLEEDS FOR YOU,

Sion

Photograph by Harrison Ashford

Renee McElrath, age 4

ISIS

I've known a woman
who traveled through the
hidden portal,
communed with the gods
and laughed at the mortals.
She was a priestess
on this soil, goddess in the heavens;
invoke her name
and she'll guide you into heaven.

In her bosom lay the sacred word,
wisdom is 20/20,
hence her visions are never blurred.
Don't know if you ever heard,
but she often transfigures into a bird.

Transmitting in the mental,
she takes refuge in the Temple.
She is beauty,
her heart is in her dimple.
Mother of all creation,
through her
I passed through the mystic initiation;
concept kematian.
Wisdom I hunger.
Knowledge is power,
and the power made me stronger.

I AM SION

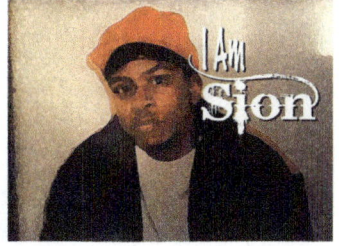

See I derived from the primordial sea,
I am more like the proverbial key.
When it comes to her,
I place none above her.
Isis is unlike any other.
She was the virgin before the virgin.
She is the holy mother.

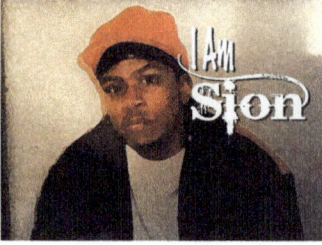

ZODIAC LOVE

I was birthed by a Taurus
who fell in love with a Libra,
rise of a Scorpion,
celestial believer.
Aries was my first love,
thought it was forever,
but she had eyes for Cancer,
her moves were real clever.

I moved on with my life,
Virgo was my next.
Never been with a virgin,
so I was anxious for the sex.
Eventually she became my ex.
Too much drama, too much pain,
plus I failed to notice that Sagittarius
was out for the same.
I proceeded with eyes
on Gemini.
Ego like Leo, was confused
and conceited.
Capricorn was envious and
thought I couldn't see it.

I AM SION

With no celestial love,
I started to feel lifeless
'til I caught the visual
of a Pisces.
I swear the value
of that moment was priceless!
Loyal like Nefertari,
with the glow of Isis.
But I never knew what passion was
'til I drank from the Aquarius
and found
that ZODIAC LOVE!

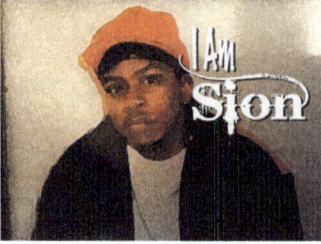

HE

He loved women,
but he beat them too.
I said, *He* loved women,
but *he* beat them too.

Smack! Strangle!
Just some of the things *he* would do.
He too was a child of neglect,
so all *he* knew was go for the neck!

Backhand smack—
he really gets going
when *he* gets crack!
He got drunk—she was there.
When *he* got back,
he said, *she* said—*he* attacked!
Front kick thrust right into her back!

Manhood *he* lacks.
To hit her as if
he were pounding a mat!
Afterward *she* cried,
and again he lied—
"Baby, I love you.
It won't happen again!"

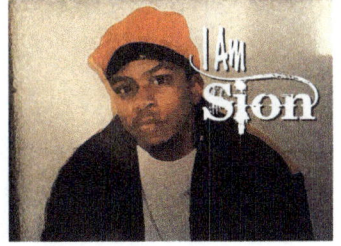

Well, next time had come and gone,
and *he* had whipped her again.
He sung the same song;
he wasn't a man.
She was fed up,
and she had a plan—
knife to his throat,

he wouldn't hurt her again!
His actions weren't loving,
so *he* got what he had coming!

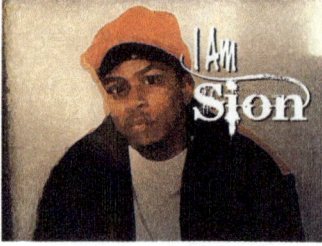

SHE

She loved him, but
she didn't realize how deep!
I said,
she loved him, but
she didn't realize how deep!
She tolerated and endured
the punches to the head and the slaps to the cheek.

She grew up in a house
without a father,
so *she* sought love from men
with whom *she* shouldn't have bothered.
She was looking for that missing love
between daddy and daughter.

She couldn't see it!
They said *he* was no good,
but *she* didn't believe it.
As for loving another man, well,
she just couldn't conceive of it.
Despite *his* cheating and drug usage,
and *she* didn't agree with it.

I AM SION

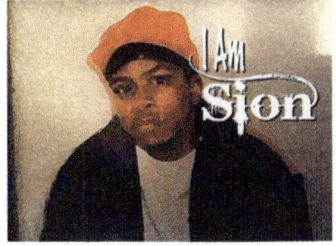

He would say sorry,
and *she'd* take him back
every time.
Then *he* would drink up
and steal *her* very last dime.

Until that next time came
when he sought to inflict pain.
She moved swiftly to his neck,
in one motion *he* lay dead.
She had no regrets,
and most would say,
that's what *he* gets!

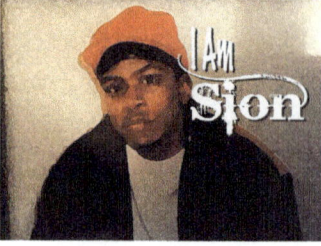

LOVE

What do you do
when a love that was whole
fragments into pieces?
When love is not expressed,
love then decreases.
Love is inspiration,
it can be both
impulsive and patient.
Some say it's a disease,
while others enjoy it with ease.
Love can bring a giant to his knees.
Love varies in all
stages and degrees.
To love
is not what you're thinking of.
To love doesn't mean that you're
in love.
Love for the moment
can change in a second.
Love can betray you
only if you let it.
Love is a cold feeling
that can warm the whole body.
I said,
Love is a cold feeling
that can warm the whole body.
Some are grateful for it,
but it's not meant for just anybody.

My Love, your Love, our Love.
Love is the source of creation.
When created in the image of God,
it's love plus motivation.

Undying love?
That kind of love is amazing,
makes you wanna hug somebody!
Smile for me if you love somebody!

SUBCONSCIOUS THOUGHT

I couldn't sleep last night—
dreamt of a past night.
Eyes wouldn't open,
I couldn't wake.
There I laid,
subconsciously seeing my face.

Walking in the mist,
saw a shadow to my left.
The air reeked of a smell—
the order of evil,
the scent of death.
The subconscious too deep,
feels too real,
I can't sleep.

Demons on my back,
casting curses in my ears.
Subconsciously feeling
the pull of my tears.
Then my eyes opened,
and nothing was lost,
but the newly gained fear
of my subconscious thoughts.

SELF VS. ELSE

I must admit I love myself,
so I could not care less
about everyone ELSE.
ELSE don't have
the best interests of SELF.
SELF does for SELF,
it's self-explanatory,
so I shouldn't have to say
nothing ELSE.
ELSE will kill you if there's
nothing ELSE to break you,
and there's always
someone ELSE to hate you.
It's best to keep distance
between SELF and ELSE.

Now all ELSE is history,
so I'm pointing at you—
'Cause if SELF is "I,"
then ELSE is "YOU"!
Know that ELSE won't care for SELF
the same as ELSE cares for you;
I mean cares for HIM!
All I got is SELF,
so I don't deal with ELSE.
Or should I say deal with THEM?
If you pose a threat to SELF,
I'll do you like I've done
no one ELSE.

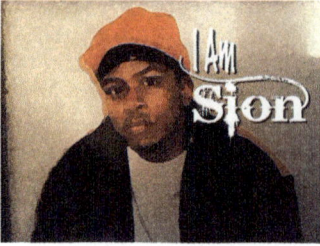

WHAT IS POETRY?

Poetry is the conversation
with the essence,
mental contemplations manifested
into verbal expressions.
Poetry is the smell,
touch, and taste,
the divine scripture
that your soul chooses to embrace.

Poetry for me
is the channeling of energy.
From symbolic parables
to speaking literally,
it's the glimpse of
the magi and star.
Or simply can be described
as the feeling you get
when buying your first car.
It's this for them
and that for someone else;
it's love and hate
intertwined in one.

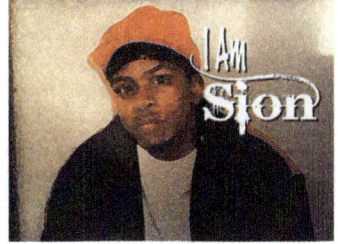

WHAT IS POETRY?

It's the passion you feel,
the perfect silence of the mind.
It's where the water is still,
and where the wind tends
to whisper in your ear.
Poetry is that smile,
but it can also be that fear.
Poetically speaking,
poetry is learning and teaching.
Poetic thoughts can never die,
as long as they breathe.

Between you and I,
WE ARE POETRY!

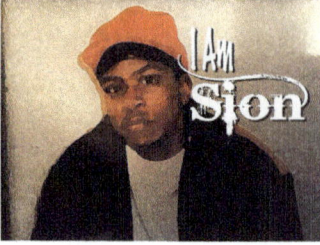

EGYPT REMEMBERED

Dark corridors, torch lit;
keepers of the amulet.
Hieroglyphics scribed on the tablet;
ESOTERIC.
Don't confuse it with magic.
The love I express for EGYPT
is deeper than any habit.
The continuance of remembrance,
Greek stagnation,
Roman hindrance.
Have you forgotten about Nubian pyramids?
Africa—a raped mother to lost kids.
The mind's eye is
deeper than an ILLUMANATIS
when they commune and chant
to the sacred goddess.
HONEST.
His third eye sees through the onyx;
meditating, medicated from
the kemetic tonic.

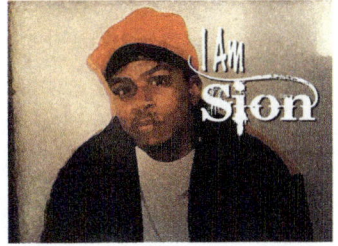

THOUGHTS OF TIFFANY

A girl no older than fifteen;
women twice her age ain't seen what she's seen.
Yet all alone, she did what she done;
Tiffany is a product of where she's from.

Opportunities evade her,
good fortune seems not to exist.
She cries herself to sleep,
nails into her palm with a clutched fist.

She can't believe her own mother
would sell her own daughter for drugs.
She can't seem to find God
where he usually was,
'cause church
ain't the same no more!

For her age, Tiffany's nobody's fool,
but her grades began to drop in school.
Teachers noticed,
but they ain't paid enough to comment,
the sickening truth
makes you want to vomit.

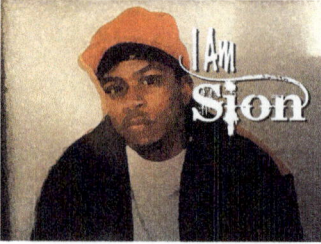

Tiff turned to the streets,
gave the wrong man a sample;
I guess her mother led
by perfect example.
Where was her father
during this rough time?
Shit! Doing rough time!
I'm talking down the creek,
around the bend and upstate;
so another shattered home
has produced nothing but hate!

At least that's what Tiffany thought!

CHESS

My territory consists
of an eight-block radius.
I'm royalty in that land,
Queen by my side,
with a scepter in my hand.

Sixty-four potential chances to lose,
because each move jeopardizes my life.
I explore the art of chess
because it's a reflection of my life.

I don't honor crooks,
I travel with bishops,
secured by rooks.
My knights are my shooters,
moving unorthodox.
Expert marksman
sounds like a paradox.

Paradoxical,
my team moves through
the opposition's obstacles,
making the impossible—possible.
The lines are drawn,
the first line of defense is the pawns.

The king can't depend
on the comfort of his team,
because if his team takes the fall,
then it's death to the king.
His vision has to be bigger
than a dream,
facts must be weighed.

My life is like chess,
but we play for keeps, not for trade.
The king's life must always be saved.
Off to the castle
when it's time for it—
sacrifice—
my rooks are ready to die for it.

I hope their death isn't in vain,
some play for their lives,
others consider it a pawn.
Until second nature takes over,
and you look over your shoulder—

CHECK MATE!
GAME OVER!

Chapter 4

Education Is Power

"It's better to die up on your feet
than to live upon your knees!"

—Emiliano Zapata

Educational Deception

Dear Parents:

I construct these words only to build an understanding with you. I want to address the educational system of the inner-city public schools, which for the sake of this scribe, I'll refer to as the "Urban School System." I claim that our children are not being properly educated. I'm not accusing any particular school. However, the vast majority may find this writing to be relatable.

Education is the natural connectivity to what was, what is, and what is yet to come. I say that education is meant to bring out the dormant potential that lies within the students, your children. Education should extract the subjective and objective qualities that the students naturally possess. However, in our Urban School System, I argue that the current standards are not bringing out that potential, but rather forcing it back in.

Therefore, the students, your children, can only recite what they've been told to memorize, ergo a parrot culture has arisen. The result is that students become "parrots," in other words, merely imitating and mimicking what they hear and see without any understanding or comprehension as to why. We must demand reform in order to ensure that students are being adequately educated, instead of trained.

We face a myriad of conundrums in addressing the defects of our Urban School System, including the following:

1. Lack of funding.
2. Curriculum that does not suit the cultural and social needs of today's youth.
3. Teachers who fail to pass competency exams in their field of study.
4. Overcrowded classrooms.
5. Lack of educational stimulation.

In addition, it seems as if our Urban School System doesn't cohesively educate as a whole, but rather enforces conformity and encourages repetitive compliance to their methodologies of human programming.

The end result is the decimation of the natural creativity, inquisitiveness, and mental elevation of the students, while at the same time failing miserably to inject a love for, and need of, a proper education.

Our educational centers have become training camps. They're not teaching the children, they're training parrots. If you expect more, do more! In today's world, the teachers' paychecks are more significant than the children's development.

Move for change! Move for action! Not tomorrow, not next week, TODAY!

Be educated!

SION

POWER

The revolution inflames me,
I wouldn't have it any other way.
I insist, revolutionary deployment,
rebel and resist. Nothing short of our life
is what we risk.
Whereby,
we struggle today for tomorrow's bliss.
I heard the cry for order, I wait for action,
execute karma for Malcolm-X and George Jackson.
I'm immersed in the study of a panther,
my fist was raised before I was out of my Pampers.
Before I could talk, I was screaming,
"Power to the people!"
When I was fourteen, I was fighting for freedom;
they had me entombed in a concrete casket.
Manhood tested, I passed it!
POWER!
I was educated on Newton,
Seale, and Clever.
Bobby Gore and Father Neil
were my teachers.
Marcus Garvey and Drew Ali
were my leaders.
ALMIGHTY!
I personify the words of Jesus,
I rebuke Babylonians,
Greeks, and Roman Caesar.
This revolution I devour, as
I am the embodiment
of all things!
POWER TO THE PEOPLE!

TRUTH SEEKER

Moorish sun
casting light on Moorish science;
defiance.
To any measure leaving my people economically dying,
far from a racist, but in me my pride is strong.
Every time I speak, it's likely about my own;
I'm so in love with mine,
there's no time to try and hate another kind.
Now comprehend this resilience,
four hundred plus years
they've been trying to strip me of my brilliance.
If you're a TRUTH SEEKER,
then I suggest you listen.
Masons wearing our fez
without permission,
they know it for themselves
that they've stolen the legacy
of our Moorish traditions.
Shriners are imposters,
learning as Muslims,
teaching as Christians.
Yet my vision remains constant,
spirit of the pharaohs
with my eyes on the Aten.
What about Amen?
Rays of the sun—Ray reflected,
forefathers thoughts—resurrected,
Scripture dissected.

Constantine deception, finally correct,
rise against the ILLUMINATION!
Can't believe that I said it,
Templars wishin'
I was beheaded.
Vice-versa,
I'm a TRUTH SEEKER,
walk the path of a holy man.
Before Is*Ra*El
Egypt was the holy land,
Ethiopia was the holy land.

Long live Nubia!
Spirits cast into the meekness.
Either you're pacified, or you're a
TRUTH SEEKER!

THE DECEPTION

Faced with the same conundrum,
old Roman crisis,
like Constantine deception,
still searching for what Christ is.
My opinion half truth, half invention.
Of course, Michelangelo needs to be mentioned.
Gave us a reflection of a white Jesus,
no coincidence that what the Holy See
is modern Roman Caesars—
wasn't Jesus from Jerusalem?

No offense, but I was
deceived by Christian leaders
who didn't know or forgot
about the Council of Nicaea.

Crucifixion, some called it crucifixion,
but we've become
too arrogant to listen.
Mother caught the Holy Ghost,
told her it was voodoo,
infiltrated during slavery,
subconscious referencing Ju-Ju.

Church on Sunday—
truly the sun's day.
Open your mind—
it was designed for Apollo.
So is it Christ
or the deception that you follow?

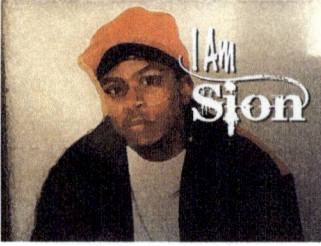

WORD IS

They ransacked ancient
temples and tombs—
where's the treasure at?
The arsons hid it in allegory,
I'm here to bring it back.
I'll die before I stop searching for it,
no matter where it's at.
I don't care what god you worship,
it won't convince me to cease my searches;
whether you're adorned with a crucifix
or travel to Mecca
to complete your circuits.
Truthfully, Immanu-El's identity
hasn't been found in the churches,
Nicean Creed you purchased.

WORD IS

Bodies laid waste
beneath Solomon's temple;
searching for wisdom
already retained in the mental.
I've been taught
by master minds
from ancient ages,
from Levite priests
to Egyptian sages.
Pentacle on my pendant,
Into Judas I will never turn—if I said it, I meant it.
Don't confuse it with demented—
wisdom speaks,
I should be commended.

108

WORD IS

Eden is where the Kurds live,
meditating on a different plain.
Show me where the earth is
and I promise,
Genesis can't teach me what birth is.

Some say I'm the truth that's been kept,
and you Romans are the
real reason why Jesus wept.
WORD IS

THINKING MAN

I've known a traveling man
who journeyed from the East.
A reflection of the sun,
to the gods he would often speak.
From beneath the sands,
he would recite and decipher the sphinx,
for he understood that they fear
the man who knows how to think.

I AM THAT I AM

I am that I am.
I've always been who I AM.
He who spoke to the burning bush,
call me the son of Cush.
Shush!
It's like it's been kept hidden.
Question—
what's the purpose of living?

I AM THAT I AM.
I've always been who I AM.
Many wives have I,
construct this temple for
the most high, said I.
For JAH I made many believers,
and Menyelik
was my seed through the Queen of Sheba.

I AM THAT I AM
I've always been who I AM.
First breath on Earth,
righteous by Nature,
royal from birth.
I was born that I AM;
surely I AM that I AM.
A student of wisdom,
a genuine TRUTH SEEKER.
I AM THAT I AM—
my brother and sister's keeper.

TRUTH BE TOLD

Dominant DNA,
I'm not recessively made weak.
This poem here may offend you
Romans and Greeks.
This is for Nubian pharaohs
and Moorish sheiks:
There will no longer be any
turning of the cheek.
What you sow, so shall you reap!

TRUTH BE TOLD

I've not forgotten,
in my silence I've been plottin'
the vengeance of an oppressed people.
European equality doesn't mean equal;
at least not for you and I—
look at how they treat you.

TRUTH BE TOLD

If the TRUTH BE TOLD,
it's not for sale, it can't be sold—
only extended this poem is Asiatic intended,
'cause I relate and feel the pain,
humility is now second nature;
I felt the shame,
you and I are one in the same.

112

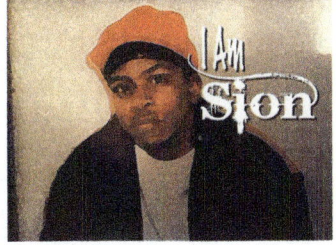

TRUTH BE TOLD

TRUTH BE TOLD!
My history is told to be true,
so in the time of war
it'll unite me and you.

DIVINE LORD

In my heart is inscribed the divine crest,
poetry is the manifestation
of your intellectual prowess.
Know this—
I'm not like many,
I am the Lord incarnate
with the spirit of Jah in me.
The preacher's pulpit pimped me,
as if the fathers didn't send me.
This is spoken word!
So cogitate circumspective
the words that I speak.
With one word I give life
when the mind's eye seems bleak.
Birthed almighty
I love Haile Selassie,
I am a divine lord,
infused with Rastafari.
The flesh may fall,
but the spirit will not die,
in the hearts of the solid
does Neil Wallace lie.

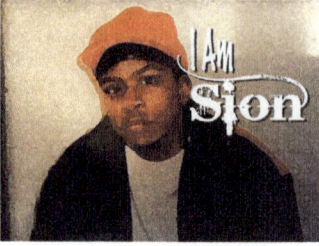

I'LL PRAY TOMORROW

Who has such time for
Asonai, Jesus, or Apollo?
Work needs to be done,
so I'll pray tomorrow.
I would have prayed today
if I was troubled with sorrow,
but since I'm not, come back and
we'll pray tomorrow.

It doesn't matter, it seems
my prayers are ignored,
and talking to myself
tends to make me bored.
I feel like I've just been conned;
if Jesus is on the main line
why doesn't he respond?

I'm behind in bills,
a car note I need to pay;
they'll repossess it
no matter how hard I pray.
I've not given up,
just come back tomorrow.
For now I got things to do,
so I'll pray tomorrow.

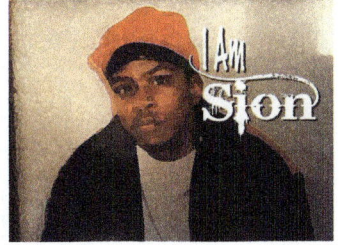

GIVE ME FREEDOM OR GIVE ME DEATH!

If your principles dictate peace,
then justice must be your cause.
We do not fight for justice
until we're assured that peace
will be our resolve.

GIVE ME FREEDOM OR GIVE ME DEATH!
Only God gives me breath.
I inhale the spirit, exhale the power.
Make divine motion as a silent angel
until my last hour.

GIVE ME FREEDOM OR GIVE ME DEATH!!!
Meditation, ascension into heaven,
some pray on ten, while
others merely salute with seven.
True angels have not wings,
don't be deceived by the reverend.

GIVE ME FREEDOM OR GIVE ME DEATH!
GIVE ME FREEDOM OR GIVE ME DEATH!
This I'll cry 'til there's no struggle left!
GIVE ME FREEDOM OR GIVE ME DEATH!
These are the only two options left.

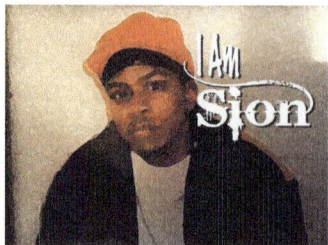

Angel

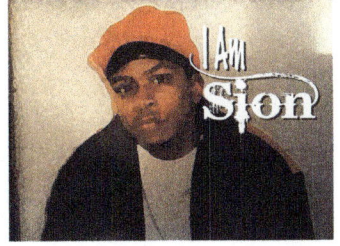

Chapter 5

Consideration

"The philosopher contemplates ideas;
the teacher energizes ideas;
the student generates ideas."

—Lionel Crocker

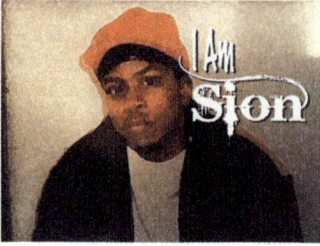

A Letter to President Barack Obama

My recollection of your 2008 campaign and election vividly etched into the very fabric of my psyche. I have consumed the pages of history regarding Africans in America, our arrival, our struggle, the digression and progression. From the moment our ancestors exited the door of no return—to the moment you historically took the world by storm.

At present I reside in one of America's many modern-day plantations—prison. Even behind these walls, you could hear the chants and cheers each time your speeches were televised. We knew then that the time for change was upon us; not just for the ills of society, but specifically for the condition of us prisoners. We had hope that the overtly racist regime of the prisons' administration would diminish, that the mysterious deaths of prisoners would end; yet, to our astonishment, they have persisted.

The expectations of you were through the roof, not only society, but in the prisons. We all looked to you for a sense of hope and direction.

I'll be bold enough to say that we the people are at fault. We focused too much attention on you and the White House. We should have invested that time, energy, and finance in other avenues of change; yet the White House was in our reach!

In focusing only on the White House on Pennsylvania Avenue, we forgot about the white houses on the corners of Watts and Compton, neglected the white houses in Harlem, ignored the white houses in Lawndale, burned the white houses on 7-Mile

118

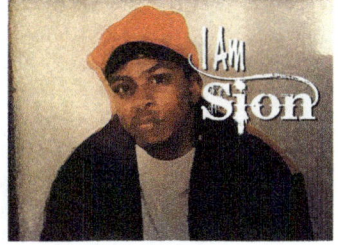

in Detroit, tore down the white houses in Muskegon Heights, Michigan. We ultimately failed ourselves and our people.

Your daughters will have the best education and will be exposed to a lifestyle that will—hopefully—better them so that in ten to fifteen years they can come among us and finish what you started and make our dreams a reality.

No Love Lost,
No Love Gained.

Michelle Obama 4-President!

MS. KATRINA
PART I

We ignored the realization, failed to see who this was—
a sister we was facing!
Should've applied the unwritten lesson—RUN!—
when a sister's built up aggression.

This Black woman wasn't playing, far from teasing.
It must've been that time of the month—excuse me—Season!
Allow me to speak for the masses, I recommend that sister take
anger-management classes!

Stirred in the Atlantic passage, voices of slaves in her mist,
she reached back and swung with a clutched fist—
somebody truly had that sister pissed!

She hit houses, stores, even arenas, but Bush blew the levees
and tried to blame it on Ms. Katrina.
She didn't care about race or kind, her journey was set,
she had only destruction on her mind.

New Orleans hasn't been the same since, so as I close,
I hope Ms. Katrina doesn't take offense.

MS. KATRINA
PART II

That sister came and was gone like a thief in the night,
if I hear raindrops I can't even sleep in the night.
Hey, Ms. Katrina, Good Riddance.
You brought nothing but pain and sickness.
It's been years since you left me, feels like a lifetime.

I AM SION

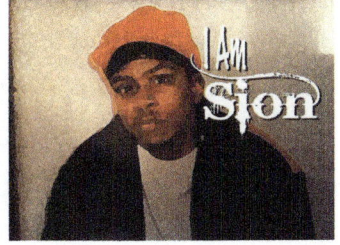

In your absence
FEMA's been having a good time profiting from our losses,
had us abandoned on top of houses.
—Nauseous—
My kufi's in the water, right next to their crosses;
Jesus pieces everywhere, but no red crosses.
—Damn!—

George Bush crossed us! Certain rappers used the flood
of the Fifth Ward to fill the city with dope.
Then Ms. Katrina flooded and the people lost hope.
Entertainers talked good on TV,
Sean Penn was saving lives in his motorboat.
Some gave money, but no physical time.
Our people went hungry
while they made sure they're bling shined.
What were you doing when the flood came?
Probably in Miami making it rain.
What, you forgot?
Well, I remember what happened.
How could you ever forget how that sister was actin'?
Whippin' her hair, tongue lashin!
Haven't seen her since,
she must have taken
those anger-management classes.
Let us pray.
Pray for the children who lost their mother and father;
pray for those souls who didn't emerge from the water.
Need we say more?
Indeed! Pray for those lost who we still light candles for.

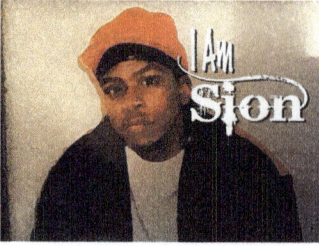

SPEAK #1

Divine Lord, embodiment
of he who created me,
prayed for my demise,
truth is why they hated me.

From pharaohs to savages,
from royalty to slaves;
to being subject to those
who once inhabited the Caucus Caves.

We forgot
that which we had already forgotten,
spiritual malady, no identity.
Lost our nationality,
and we can't see
that the holy breath still exists,
nor that Immanu-El's paradise
is merely mental bliss.

SPEAK #2

This isn't blasphemy,
though I witnessed John when he baptized Jesus,
gave Leonardo my blessings when I viewed the Mona Lisa.
I was bewildered by Mozart, yet found joy in his tune.
The wonders of my mind, I may just be speaking too soon.
So will you decide to curse me or kill me like Socrates?
Banish me as if I'm Aristotle?
The Priest of the sun has risen, the genie is out of the bottle.
If I shall pass before I wake, promise me one thing—
I'll be buried amongst my kindred
in the ancient Valley of the Kings.

WHY?

WHY are we being systematically deceived by our schools?
WHY does the "fuck it" attitude make us so cool?
WHY?
WHY are we still dying from social stress?
WHY do we not see
we've become economically oppressed?
WHY are we still in the hood,
repin' the East or the West?
WHY don't we own that land to really contest?
WHY do we still blame those white men
when for his military you're still willing to fight?
WHY are you not concerned with your health?
WHY are you waiting on others?
WHY do you not love yourself?
WHY are you thirty and still trying to be a thug?
WHY are you not looking for black love?
Tell me—
WHY does it take Barack and Michelle
to show you what those images are?
WHY are black people so angry?
WHY am I the culprit?
Shame on me!
I'm only asking WHY?
Can you blame me?

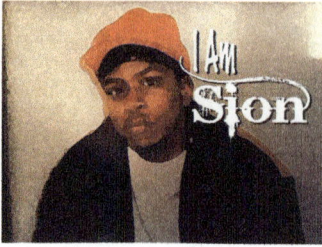

INSIGHT

Cryptic tried to decrypt the hidden cipher,
said the world would end in 2012—such liars!
Mirror our galaxy, find life just like us;
travel back through parallel dimensions
before the blood of Christ was even mentioned.
Back to when we were walking the earth land,
and God became man from intercourse
with the daughters of men,
and of course before the holy city of heaven
was sunken in sand.
Poetic prophecy, esoteric philosophy;
Greeks stole Egypt's wisdom
and put it in mythology
and didn't even say, Pardon me!
Pardon me
for speaking what's in the heart of me;
I hear them chantin',
Sion is what they're callin' me.

PARENTAGE

Bobby laid the concrete, Neil solidified it.
All descendants of his concepts and epitomized it.
Pursuing that oneness with Allah
before we even realized it.

Walt Wheat was slain untimely,
you can still hear the mourners.
He constructed the globe
and put Hustlers on each of the Four Corners.

Al-Huda is known to many,
but felt that iron hand that was shown to many.

Anybody could not have filled that void,
on this holy divine day
we give thanks to Willie Lloyd.

I came in PEACE!
Palms North, crown East.
In solidarity, solid to the T.

UNTOUCHABLE GATE

Close observation I call it the UNTOUCHABLE GATE,
THE CITY OF SAINTS, where Roman Emperors and Popes
lay esoteric lessons.
Child abuse viewed as Blessings?
Question?
Have you heard of the Catholic-Mafia Connection?

Europe in the Americas slaughtered the Indians,
the people of Israel in conflict with Palestinians;
Afghanistan, Iran, and need I say more?
North Korea, Somalia—playgrounds of war;
the Twin Towers fell,
that was a bit much.
But—the gates of the Pope
have never been touched.

I say what's needed to be, the city of secrets
is not that mysterious.
Neither is the female Pope-Pope Joan,
nor is the vault of the grail tablets of stone.
You can't believe I've implied such,
but John Paul knew why
the gates were never touched.

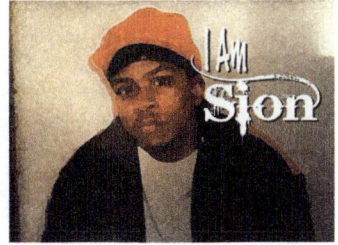

EXCOMMUNICATED

They say I'm no longer Moorish-American,
disclaimed me like swift angel's prediction.
I thought I was what I was,
beyond doubt or contradiction,
but apparently their power
extends beyond the great creator.
Drew Ali was my emancipator,
Saddi El had me believing in hope,
then Makkah Bey hung it upside down
by the rope.
What a travesty!
While I sacrificed
so others could live lavishly,
falsely accused me,
portrayed me savagely.
Too many dictators—
sorry, your majesty—
don't be mad at me!
Too much turning the other cheek,
too many national grand sheiks.
Not enough Indians to go around—
too many damn chiefs!
Disclaimed me,
like swift angel's prediction.
I thought I was what I was,
beyond doubt or contradiction.

NEVER FORGOTTEN

It started for me with Frank School,
who taught me to distinguish
the wise man from a fool.
I was raised by GHAZI,
who showed me how God see,
and who the Lord be.
Many had cast me away
as if they couldn't afford me.
I continued to reach out to Tone-X,
but it seemed he ignored me.
Passivity bored me—
maybe this is why
Malijah-X adored me.
He gave me my attribute,
I've been supreme ever since,
though it was Charles-X
who showed me how
spiritual science made sense.
Death before dishonor,
this is how I feel,
one of my greatest teachers
was Travis El.

Breathed on me the Moorish spirit,
even when I was too lost to hear it.
The wisest of men
was Amon Ra.
Thought to be crazy,
but I met a true genius
in Antonio Lacey,
and Crumb G remains
on my right side—
never behind me.
'Cause the mastermind revolutionary
refined me;
through their tutelage
it all began to make sense.
Hasan adopted me
and it's been Harlem ever since.

I am Sion

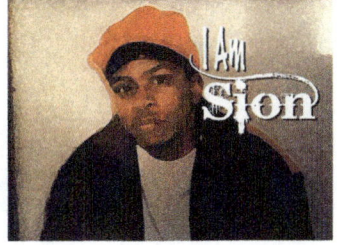

Chapter 6

Crawl Before You Walk

"Rosa Parks sat so Martin Luther King could walk.
Martin Luther King walked so Obama could run.
Obama's running so we all can fly."

—Jay-Z

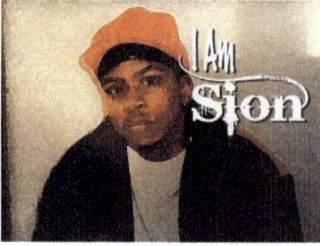

Dear World

I sit here composing this letter with the hope that you and I can come to some sort of common ground, 'cause I feel like you turned your back on me, neglected me, and kicked me when I was down. Yet you expect me to smile and be gracious. What the hell should I be grateful for? Have you heard the cries of my mother, the mourning of my soul, and the laughter of my enemies?

I was raised across the street from drugs, around the corner from murders. I attended the school of corruption and sat in a church of lies. I swam in the deep end of sorrow and slept in the company of misery. I was immersed in the atmosphere that wasn't conducive to healthy living, and I'm a product of that environment. Grateful? For what?

I sat in the courtroom of America's judicial system when I was fourteen years old. I listened intently to the legal jargon, yet was unable to comprehend its meaning; lawyers and judges speak a foreign language. I did understand the numbers, especially when the judge said eleven to forty years in prison. I heard my mother scream, saw my grandma cry, felt Shelon grab me, but the bailiffs forced my lil' cousin to release her grip from my arm as I walked past. NOW LOOK AT ME!

Prison is like high school. It's a hierarchy. You got your jocks, nerds and geeks, the popular crowd and the outcasts. No lie, it's crazy. The jocks prey on the nerds, the geeks want to be popular, and those who are popular fear that one day they may be an outcast. It's a social system, but the major difference is that it's dead!

I AM SION

I literally grew up in prison. I was raised by the hole, the box. The lessons of my life were learned through prison wars.

I was taken off the streets at fourteen, so my perception of manhood became who could fight the best, or who could disrespect and put fear in the guards the most. The prison yard became my life, and I sought to rule my life.

Now the world asks me why is it that I've become so rebellious? What other way do I know? I had no alternatives. My mentors were gang leaders, my occupation was gambling, my reality was dictated by prison politics. How can you question my sincerity in wanting to be released? There's nothing that I want more than my FREEDOM!

Yet I'm so numb. I can't even remember what FREEDOM feels like. I'm in my twenties now and have been in prison a long time, and they have been agonizing years. I don't even know how the world looks anymore. I'm sure it isn't the same as it was when I was fourteen. It's crazy! How can I fight to return home? I don't know what home is! All I know is a prison cell.

Dear world, I don't mean to sound so dramatic, but the truth is the truth. I bear a burden that mere words will never be able to describe or come close to depicting in an accurate picture. I thought I would take this time to surrender my thoughts. Hope to see you soon!

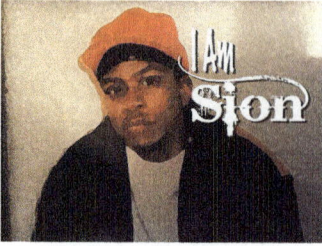

My Reflection

This morning I became conscious before my eyes even fluttered. I laid there for a while and assessed my physical form. When I finally opened my lids, I was staring up at a concrete ceiling. I inhaled and then exhaled deeply, because no matter the beauty of my dreams, I always awake to a nightmare. I lifted my back from the concrete bed frame and planted the soles of my feet on the concrete floor. I sat there for a moment, taking in the full view of my 5x9 cell, the white concrete walls, and a sense of misery swept over me.

I rose up, stretching my legs and arms, my arms nearly touching each side of the walls. I walked, more like staggered, the 2½ steps to my sink and glanced in the mirror above it, examining my refection intensely. "DAMN!" I thought as I faced the recurring reality that I was literally entombed in a concrete casket!

I looked deep into my own eyes and honestly felt as if I were looking at a stranger. My appearance didn't match the fabric of my soul. All I saw was pain and hatred. How did I get to this point? A point to where life becomes an illusion and your reality is distorted by make-believe and what not. From this point, how can I distinguish the fictitious from the absolute?

This morning I saw failure in my reflection.

SION

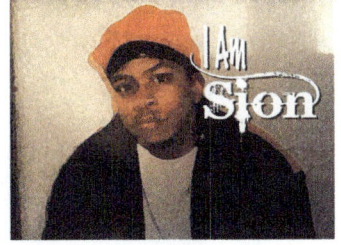

Chapter 7

Expressing Me

"Every person in the society of free nations—
and even those who are repressed
under the heels of dictators—
has a right to express his or her opinion."

—Fidel Castro

Thoughts of Sion

ON RELIGION AND SPIRITUALITY:

Spirituality is the internal alignment and connection between you and your Creator. Religion gives us ceremonies and rites to help facilitate the understanding and strengthening of our spirituality.

ON CHRISTIANITY, ISLAM, AND JUDAISM:

Each of these religions shares similar tenets and concepts, though they vary in their interpretations. This, in itself, perpetuates religious division. All men and women should be united in their pursuit to worship, serve, and labor for their God.

ON POLITICS:

Trickery! That's the first word that my thoughts are able to conjure when I hear the word *politics*.

ON WOMEN:

I think women are one of God's highest creations. In ancient times, women were revered and, often times, worshipped. They say, "Behind every great man is a great woman," but I disagree. I believe beside every great man is a great woman. Do you agree?

ON MUSIC:

Truth be told, music is like my therapy. The vibratory pitches of rheumatic cadences soothe my soul.

I AM SION

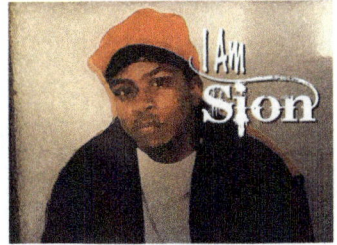

ON HIP HOP:

I love hip hop! Hip hop isn't just music—it's a culture. It's in your walk, talk, and the very fabric of your character.

ON THE MEDIA:

When you're dealing with the media, you have to be mindful of their agenda, which is often concealed. They will only tell you what they want you to know.

ON PRISON:

Prison is a modern-day slave plantation! Slave and slave master. I can only encourage all those who have their freedom to cherish it. Prison is mental and emotional torture.

ON ASSATA SHAKUR—THE EMBODIMENT OF RESISTANCE:

Africa is universally accepted as the cradle of civilization. I believe a united Africa would cause political and financial disruption in Europe and America, so it's best from both their perspectives to keep Africa divided. It's sad that even now, many people still believe Africa to be all jungles. I don't understand people's fear when it comes to raising consciousness of the ancient and modern civilization of Africa.

ON RACISM:

Racism is alive and well. Some are able to ignore it, while others are blind to it. In the end, racism is the root cause of many of today's injustices.

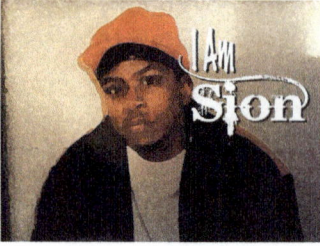

ON KHALIL GIBRAN:

In my opinion, Khalil Gibran is simply one of the greatest poets to ever touch a pen.

ON EDGAR CAYCE:

Amongst many, the *Birth of Souls* by Edgar Cayce is considered one of the most enlightening books they have ever read, myself included.

ON HARRY POTTER:

Yo! Don't disrespect Harry Potter! He's got heart! But seriously, that is the best series of books that I've ever read—I am not afraid to say it!

ON MY THOUGHTS:

MY THOUGHTS ARE BUT MY THOUGHTS—HATE THEM OR LOVE THEM!

RAPE

Up close and personal,
RAPE of Mother Afrika
came from a distance.
I'm not speaking for instance,
I'm screaming for Vengeance,
penetrated her womb
and stole her innocence.

This sister gave birth
to many Nations,
the time shall come
just have patience.

They put up obstacles,
but she went though it,
caressed her soil,
and injected hate into it,
it was simply RAPE
before she even knew it.
Today they've changed tactics,
but truly they still do it.

EVER FORGOTTEN

How can I ever forget
the likes of my Brothers,
the Brothers who gave me
Spiritual Love,
to be nobody's fool,
from Crumb-G to Frank School.

The Honor is never forgotten,
I salute you still.
My Divine Mentors Charles-X and Travis El.
This is to show my appreciation
the only real way,
so I tilt my hat to
Randal-X and R-Hollyfield Bey.

I keep ya'll in my thoughts
no matter what step is Next,
I found true master minds
in Amenra and Malijah-X.

Ghazi gave me the misson,
but I thank Hasan
for opening my eyes to the vision.
I met each of you in
the Struggles of Prison,
some Muslims, some Christians.

You Brothers strengthened me
in this life I Live,
so you're never forgotten
with this Love I give.

WORD SMITH

Say hello to the Word Smith
greetings
and know that I appreciate you
attending this verbal meeting,
meaning
your soul is what I'm reaching.
For—
Or your mental reservoir,
to say needless,
he just refused to speak
the Queen's English.

When I speak it's not periphrasis,
my vernacular surpasses
all things that it grasps.
The conqueror of
imperialistic fascist,
I digest knowledge
in reasonable rations.

Mind over matter,
suppressing my passions.
I can destroy and rebuild
with my words and actions.
Word Smith mixing words with
mortal illusions and God's Gift.

DIGEST

As of late, my struggle
has been a frequent occurrence,
currently
I've been swimming opposite
the currents.
Is he mere mortal
or more of a vicegerent?

Seeking success by
any and all means
got complex visions,
and only I can decipher
my dreams,
and it seems
my contemporaries
are all influenced
by the wrong things,
which means
their words are corrupt
and we're victims of their schemes.

I lived up the road from welfare,
across the street from poverty,
where success is a dream
and we sell misery
as a commodity.

I AM SION

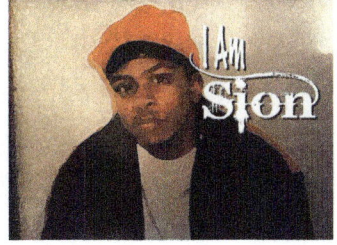

They say I've made
the impossible possible,
I'm a living anomaly.

Went to school, but
my teachers taught a fallacy,
they restricted my words
and suppressed my analogy.

So I grew up furiously,
now my pain got life,
and it's living vicariously.
I didn't come from a broken home,
but Mama had a broken marriage,
and her 14-year-old son
went to prison.
Call it judicial miscarriage.

If I can digest that,
you can digest this.

TREASON

I remember you loved me
and that love was reciprocated.
I was undoubtedly loyal
when others' loyalty was underrated.

I remember you loved me
and I loved you undyingly.
Then finally
you killed my spirits
and watched it die in me.

I remember you loved me.
Whatever happened to that Love?
That mighty Love
that Bobby spoke of,
you know
that Willie talked about,
that Wheat hustled for
and Ike sought out.

That Love that was
buried in us all.
That Rico brought out
and Mahdi made us
shout about.
But now that kind of Love
ain't even talked about.

I Loved you
and I didn't need a reason.
I gave you my life
and in return you gave me treason.
You were my priority,
I placed you before all others.
Can you imagine
what that did to my mother?

So my departure is painful,
say good-bye to a Fallen Angel.

To all the haterz who keep me motivated—Good lookin!

ENJOY

SION

I SALUTE:

Johnny Miller, Lil Ty, Cliff, Q-B, Razor, Lil Gangsta, Troy, No-limit, Short Dog, Blair, Ken, Keith, D-P, Lil' Larry, Fred Davis, D.T., Lil'B, Big Johnny, Lil'Dre, Zoe, Dale, Vito, Dizzy, Frank White, Slim, Pac, Steele, Red, 7-Mile, Travis-El, Struck, Delray Bone, Big Ced, Dark, Tip, Malijah-X, P.J., Charles-X, Kitchen-Bey, WU-X, Ray-Ray, Kindred-El, Dre Scott, Steve-X, Rimmer-Bey, J.B., Dee-Dee, Black, Smoke, Lamont-X, Cujo, Antonio-X, Tel, Bread, Mike, Marlo, D-X, Will, Bleed, Yung, Johnson Bey, Trill, Chill, Lil' Roc, Beady, Harris-Bey, Edwards-E1, Randal-X, Frank Mills, Carlito, Renegade, Crumb, Twon, OG Rock, Chi, Lean, Suge, West Warren, Fat Mike, Nardo, Rell, Poonah, Dee, Sheed Murda, Tone, Posey-Bey, Stacks, Kilo, Tax, Sa-Black, Pepin 2-Gun'z, Hood, Sunny Black, 42nd, 43rd, Fruit, Drama, Skills, Life, Jewels, Kellogg, Mull, Silva, York, Cash, Cain, Amen Ra, Spray, Playboy, O-X, Buc, M.B., Los, Dru, Lil'D, Franklin-el, Magz, Network, Spitz, Weezy, Sed, Low-Down, Shot'ta, AK, Southwest, Big Bo, Lunatik, Lil' Tommy.

With undying love to my Big Brothers
Ant-X and the Ghost of Rich Porter.
This is also to my Lil' Bro Salle.
This is for us!
Death before Dishonor.

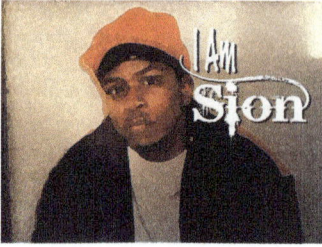

Troy and Renee McElrath

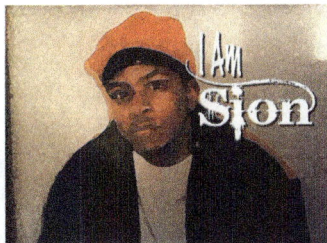

Last Wordz

A lot of people told me it would be impossible to get my book published. They say I'm not in conformity with the modern status quo that a convict such as me will always be and remain nothing but a convict. Well, now you can add author to my resume. So I guess the tide has turned and the underdog is now on the rise.

This composition is a testament that I was here, that I struggled, and that I conquered. I'm not looking to sell a million copies; I accomplished my goal already the moment the last page was completed.

For me, I feel as if I've defied people's expectations; I made the impossible possible, through God. To all those who supported this movement, I appreciate you and I refuse to let you down.

There's a campaign on the horizon. Roll with it or get rolled over.

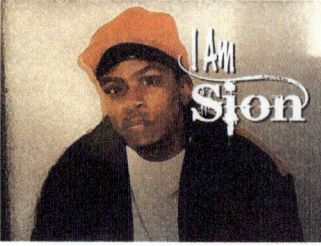

Sion is the name

and

Dream Chaserz is the Movement

Love Life

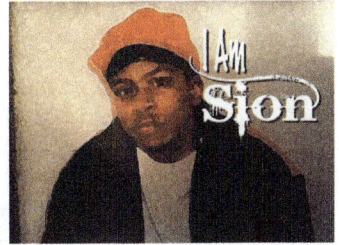

AUTHOR'S BIO

"Sion" was born William Kitchen III in the inner city of Muskegon Heights, Michigan. In 2000 Sion was incarcerated at the age of 14 and subsequently sentenced to 11-40 years in prison.

Inn 2007 Sion became the Founding Director of Sion Avenue Organization, an incorporated nonprofit charity.

He is an author of various published articles and is presently the designer and editor of *Blaze 1st*, the newsletter.

For more information write to:

Gold Ink Content
C/O I am Sion
PO Box 4663
Muskegon, Michigan 49444

Or go to:

www.facebook/iamsion.com
www.goldinkcontent.com

The following is an interview conducted in late 2012
with SION by Gold Ink Content.

I AM SION

The Interview

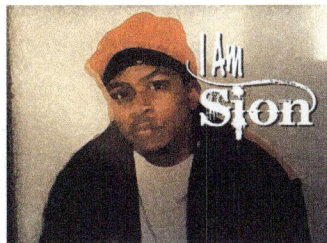

GOLD Ink Content (GIC): For those who are unaware of who you are and your struggle, will you please tell us a little about yourself?

SION: Of course. I'm called Sion. I was born William Kitchen III in Muskegon Heights, Michigan, in 1985. At the age of 14, I was incarcerated for robbery and gun chargers. I've been in prison now for over half of my life.

GIC: So that'll make you late 20s?

SION: Yeah, but I swear I feel like 47.

GIC: We've read your book, and it is evident you are a gifted poet. How long have you been writing poetry?

SION: Since I was about 7 years old. I remember being given poems to recite at church during the holiday events. I can remember always appreciating the beauty of words and how you could reach so many people with them.

GIC: So that's how it all began. In church?

SION: Indeed, a couple of years later, around the age of 9 or 10. I would be allowed to write my own poems for the events, either take a poem that was given to me and put my own spin on it.

GIC: I see. Have you ever been interested in Rap?

SION: Name me one inner-city kid that wasn't … why?

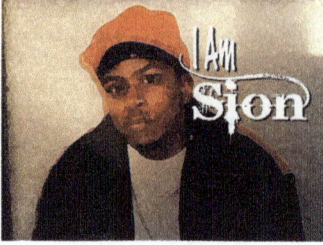

GIC: Because many people believe Rap and poetry are inter-changeable.

SION: They're differently relatable. As a kid growing up, I did have ambitions of being a Rapper. But my Mother didn't approve of my rap lyrics and forced me to write more positively. So I did. I subsequently took away the beat, slowed the verbal cadence, and added positive concepts, and out of that came poems.

GIC: Is poetry always positive?

SION: Back then, I thought so. But as I matured in poetry, I began to realize that poetry is what you make it. Rather, it can be moral or immoral, good or evil, it is your perception and expression expressed, either verbally or in written form. I simply like to consider it a "lyrical thought brought into fruition by words."

GIC: That was beautiful.

SION: Thank you.

GIC: Tell us the inspiration behind your book, *I AM SION*.

SION: I was inspired by a few different things, the first being my mother, giving her at least one thing from me that she could be proud of. The second being for the many people who are told that their dream is impossible, so I'm fueled by making the impossible possible.

GIC: How long did it take to produce your manuscript?

SION: Well, I started it in 2009, not really expecting it to take on the life that it has. Then once I decided to seek publishing avenues, I was stagnated due to my incarceration and lack of support.

GIC: I can only imagine. It must have really been a struggle.

SION: Absolutely. Especially when you factor in I've been locked up in level 5 (maximum security) for 90 percent of my life, which is 23-hour lockdown. So my access to the free world has been minimum. Not to mention how many times I've been turned down due to my inability to communicate.

GIC: How long do you have left in prison?

SION: Technically, I was scheduled to be released back in June 2011. That was the earliest release date, but due to my institutional conduct, my parole has been delayed. I should be getting out soon.

GIC: That's not bad.

SION: I beg to differ, especially when you've already done so much time.

GIC: You're right. So tell us, what we can expect from this book?

SION: Different people will walk away with different feelings. But I did try to incorporate something for everybody. I'm big on education and self-reflection, so you'll find many poems in that regard.

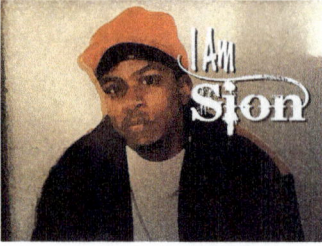

GIC: Two of my favorite poems personally are Ms. Katrina and Ms. Katrina part 2. Can you explain your state of thought at the time you wrote those poems?

SION: The first version of Ms. Katrina was written a couple of months following the hurricane itself. The news reports were never ending. Conspiracy theories were rampant, and the victims were still without adequate shelter. Lives were lost and bodies never found. So my state of thought was vengeance, but in a situation like that, who can you inflict vengeance on? Katrina isn't a person. So Ms. Katrina was intended to humanize the hurricane, to personify it as an actual person.

GIC: And what about part 2?

SION: I wrote part 2 in 2011. And after six years, New Orleans had yet to be recovered, and so many of its residents were still displaced. I wanted to illuminate the perpetual struggle. I felt like a part 2 was due, and I touched on something that I wasn't conscious of in the original version.

GIC: The poems "Dear Renee." Were those poems written from a personal perspective?

SION: Truly. In them I attempted to reveal my relationship and feelings toward my mother.

GIC: It seems as if you and your mother are extremely close. Are you secretly a Mama's boy?

SION: (smiles) Well ... I guess you can say that. I know if I say no, she'll throw a fit. The reality is, Mom is my best friend and I love her more than life itself.

GIC: (laughs) Awwww! That's so sweet.

Sion: Stop laughing at me ... shouts out to Mom.

GIC: The subtitle to *I Am Sion* is *No Better Wordz*. What does that mean?

SION: Simple. There's no better wordz to describe the love, pain, and wisdom that I impart in this book.

GIC: Cocky, aren't we.

SION: Only confident.

GIC: We've heard a rumor that you have a poem called "Poetic Prophecy" which you've kept to yourself. Do you have such a poem?

SION: I do.

GIC: What is it about?

SION: Life and death.

GIC: Can you share more with us about it?

SION: Nope.

GIC: Well, can you at least tell us when we can look forward to reading it?

SION: You may hear it first, so just stay tuned.

GIC: All right, we will let you slide on that. Is there anything you'd like to add before we conclude this interview?

SION: Just read the book. No Better Wordz can describe my appreciation.

GIC: We truly wish you much success.

SION: Before we part. Look out for Randal-X. He is up next. Followed by DeCarlose "Crumb" Smith. This isn't just about me. This is a movement and we mean to M O V E. This is our year and I promise you, you won't be disappointed by our Works.

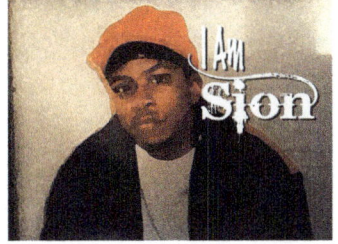

WORDZ

To those who saw me on the rise
and tried to pull me down,
how do the bottoms of my shoes look?

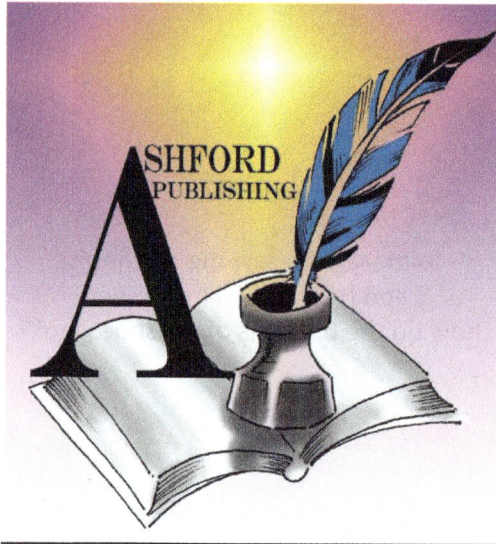

The goal of Ashford Publishing is to publish literature
that adds integrity to the global society,
with books that reflect enlightenment
and inspirational thought,
and poetry and fiction that have
elements of authenticity.

As the O'Jays say, "We have a message in our writings."

CPSIA information can be obtained at www.ICGtesting.com
Printed in the USA
BVOW10s2353300713

327397BV00003B/4/P

9 780976 990154